D1391443

FAKEAWAY
MANUAL

FAKEAWAY
MANUAL

CREATING YOUR FAVOURITE
TAKEAWAY DISHES AT HOME

FERGAL CONNOLLY
PHOTOGRAPHS BY NICKI DOWEY

CONTENTS

Introduction

Today, the popularity of the takeaway owes its success to many modern technological and social influences. These range from the demise of the traditional family set-up and a rise in single-dweller living to greater demand for convenience coupled with an upwelling of interest in food and an insatiable appetite for a huge variety of different cuisines – all of which can be ever-more easily ordered and delivered via sophisticated technology.

THE HISTORY OF THE TAKEAWAY

Although many may think of the takeaway as a modern phenomenon that dates back to the advent of the motor car or even the smartphone, it is of course far, far older than that. In fact, the practice of taking food away or having it delivered has been around since early civilisation, when many people bought the majority of their meals from stalls at markets since they didn't have the facilities at home to cook for themselves. There is much evidence for this, in art and literature as well as in physical form in Pompeii, where the preserved remains of food stalls can be found among the ruins.

Looking back into culinary history, there are a number of significant milestones that helped accelerate the demand for food that could either be taken away from the home or bought and consumed on the hoof. These include the movement of people to the New World in the 16th century – from the initial travellers from Spain and Italy to the migrants who built the cities of the east coast of the USA – all of whom brought with them their country's dishes and ways of cooking and eating and adapted them to the ingredients that were available to them. As these disparate cultures and cuisines melded together, so were born takeaway classics such as chop suey, Tex-Mex, nachos and countless other fusion foods.

The middle of the 20th century saw a real acceleration in the popularity of fast food as we know it today. Suburban post-war boomers with two cars and more leisure time (spent watching television) and disposable income than their parents' generation were targeted via TV adverts to have take-out food at home, whether bought from restaurants or delivered to their door. As people spent more time commuting to and from work, so the drive-in restaurant and the 'food on the go' movement arose, as convenience became king.

As supermarkets took over from independent grocers and more households owned a microwave, the market in ready meals boomed as cash-rich, time-poor households struggled to find time to make the old favourites themselves. Often laden with salt, additives and ingredients of dubious provenance, these early ready meals slowly evolved to meet the more stringent demands of their consumers, and today the chilled aisles of supermarkets are heaving with dishes from around the world that range from pig-out feasts to healthy-eating hits. Stores are also increasingly trying to mirror what you would get at your local restaurant by offering multi-dish meal deals, which essentially involve you reheating a number of foods that have been cooked days in advance. No matter how hard the product developers try, it is pretty much impossible to recreate the freshness, flavour and punch of authentic gutsiness of the real deal when you have to make it en masse and then package, distribute and store it on supermarket shelves.

The next major advance occurred in the middle of the 1990s as the internet was starting to make its mark. Restaurants could now post their menus online so customers could instantly access them, and as the technology improved, online ordering systems became the norm. These spread and improved rapidly, and today all it takes is one touch on a food delivery app for you to be able to access dishes from countless local restaurants offering foods from around the world. As this technology advances further, and more and more food is delivered by drone or driverless vehicles, summoning food that someone else has prepared is inevitably going to become even easier. But at what cost?

all of the processes. Ditto the prep time, although proving and marinating times are listed separately, and timings for procedures such as preparing a barbecue are not explicitly stated since they can vary. These timing guidelines are intended to help you plan, rather than being hard-and-fast rules: every cook works at a different pace, after all.

CIY (COOK-IT-YOURSELF)

For all that they are convenient, there is little doubt that some takeaway foods are at best simply an expensive way to eat and at worst unhealthy, unethical and unappetising. The reason for writing this book is to try to give you the tools to make a variety of your favourite takeaway dishes for yourself, using top-quality, ethically-sourced ingredients, for less than you would pay in your local food-delivery joint. Rather than your meal arriving in a slightly crushed, distressed and perspiring state you'll be able to eat fresh food that has been freshly cooked in your own kitchen. You will notice the differences in both taste and texture as the inevitable element of delay involved with having food delivered is removed from the equation: no more tepid, soggy pizzas or sweaty chips in their condensation-forming packaging.

I faced a dilemma when writing, about whether or not the recipes should be made in the traditional way, using the methods of a commercial kitchen, or adapted to suit the home cook. I decided that, where possible, I'd suggest using modern domestic appliances, none of which are overly specialist or unusual, and have created a kit list to guide you. It's not entirely necessary to have everything, but there's no doubt that certain pieces of equipment will make your life easier, the recipes faster and essentially give you an authentic takeaway look and flavour.

I've tried to include dishes suitable for various times of the day, from breakfast to a late-night snack, as well as choosing ones from a wide range of different countries. It pays to read the recipe through before you even start to think about making it, taking note of the cooking and preparation times and ensuring you plan ahead accordingly. When several things occur simultaneously, such as cooking some noodles while a sauce is bubbling away, the cooking time will cover only the longer cooking time, which encompasses

Ingredients are listed in the order in which they appear in the method, but don't presume that all of an ingredient is used at its first mention in the method. Really take the time to read through the instructions first so you are clear in your mind about what you need to add when, and how much. Some recipes are definitely more difficult than others, and the pan 🍳 rating gives you an indication of how involved the processes may be. Sometimes a recipe, such as fries, may be fairly simple to prepare but requires deep-frying, which is a potentially dangerous technique and should always be done very carefully. Others may not be dangerous but do involve a lot of stages, such as making pastry, so again these are marked with more pans than a dish that involves only the most basic chopping and stirring.

A NOTE ABOUT CURRY

No other cuisine has had more of an impact on the UK takeaway scene than curry – the popularity of which remains unrivalled. Although some dishes remain authentic to their country of origin, many British favourites are hybrids that were developed to suit the tastes of their new audience. Two of the most famous of these are chicken tikka masala, with its tomato-soup sauce, and the infamous super-hot vinadaloo curry, which is an Anglicised version of a Goan pork curry, the *vin* meaning 'wine' and the *aloo* meaning 'garlic'. Where this lads'-night-out super-hot curry came from remains something of a mystery, but the fact of its existence and continued popularity just goes to show how food culture evolves to meet the needs of locals and just how adaptable cooking is.

1. A good-quality long, serrated bread knife. Keep it solely for bread and it will cut even the crustiest of loaves for many years. You only need a couple of other sizes of knives for most things – the key is to make sure they are sharp and comfortable to hold.

2. A simple speed peeler does what is says and also makes ribbons of vegetables in seconds.

3. A microplane grater is always handy so you can grate on the move rather than being fixed to one spot, as you are with a box grater. If you can, buy several in different grades so you can grate everything from cheese to nutmeg.

4. A mandolin to shred and chop like a pro. These are dangerous bits of kit and can easily slice off the side of your thumb, so always use the guard and extreme caution. If in doubt, stick with the chopping blade on a food processor or a sharp knife.

5. A food processor with interchangeable blades so you can chop, grate and shred. Mini food processors are especially useful for whizzing up small quantities and making cooking pastes.

6. A blender, for drink and liquids such as soups and sauces, gives you a much smoother texture than a food processor.

7. A stick blender is extremely useful for quickly and cleanly pulverising smaller quantities of ingredients to a smooth sauce.

8. A stand mixer or hand mixer is extremely useful for making all kinds of batters, whisking egg whites and, if they come with a dough hook, kneading dough. The former is preferable but can be expensive, while the latter is more portable and cheaper.

9. A deep-fryer is a safe, controllable way of frying food. Buy one with a removable insert tray that holds the oil since this will make cleaning a cinch – you'll wonder why you never had one before (maybe). If you prefer not to buy one then you can use a large, deep pan instead, although it will be neither as easy to control nor as safe to use. Take great care when lowering in and removing food, using a slotted spoon, and make sure you use a thermometer to constantly check the oil isn't getting too hot. It's also a good idea to use an extractor fan at the same time to avoid the cooking smell dispersing throughout the house.

10. A mortar and pestle is useful for those little jobs the food processor can't handle, or simply for ease if you can't be bothered to get the processor out of the cupboard. Try to find a natural stone one with rough edges to help grind smoothly – generally the heavier the better. Many Asian supermarkets sell them at reasonable prices.

11. A barbecue with a lid and tongs is so useful and will enable you to cook almost anything – from pulled pork to pizza.

12. A pizza stone is a ceramic slab that when placed into an oven or on to a barbecue can absorb heat and give a pizza a genuinely great crispy crust. A very heavy baking sheet (preferably made from copper!) can give similar results.

13. A pizza peel is a giant paddle used for sliding pizzas on to or off a pizza stone (or a wood-fired pizza oven, should you have one). You can use a rimless baking sheet or thin chopping board instead.

14. Flat metal skewers, for tandoori or kebabs, are easier to use that bamboo ones since they don't need soaking and won't char. Reusable too!

15. A large wok is perfect for stir-frying and can be used for deep-frying, too. Try to get a flat-bottomed one so you don't have to have a holder to keep it level on the hob. A large frying pan will do, at a pinch, although it won't hold as much or cook the food as evenly.

16. A deep-pan pizza pan is handy if you plan to make lots. Otherwise a heavy cake tin (pan) will do.

17. Weighing scales and measuring spoons are really important for some recipes, especially breads, cakes and cookies, when it really does matter how much of each ingredient you use.

18. A selection of large and small mixing bowls, chopping boards and wooden spoons are a must.

19. Various spatulas, for scraping the dregs out of mixing bowls. Try to buy heatproof ones as they are infinitely more useful.

20. Cranked hamburger turner or a stainless-steel spatula. Very handy pieces of kit that can be used for easing pizzas out of pans as well as flipping burgers!

21. Old takeaway containers and zip-lock bags are invaluable for storing foods in the fridge, freezer or out on the counter. They are also great for marinating.

22. Empty jars and bottles are perfect for all your home-made sauces, pickles and chutneys. Sterilisation couldn't be easier (see page 16).

23. You have a phone; it probably has a timer on it! If not, use the one on your oven or buy one.

Sources of Ingredients

Below are a couple of places in which I like to buy ingredients, but if you have a local store do approach them and ask them to order a special ingredient or some different fruits and vegetables. A lot of foody storekeepers and stall holders are very proud of what they do and will be delighted to show you their wares and take on the challenge of making or sourcing new products.

Amazon For equipment, dried food and fresh food products – and just about everything else in between. www.amazon.co.uk

Lakeland A one-stop shop for all manner of cooking utensils, gadgets and appliances. www.lakeland.co.uk

Sage Beautifully designed kitchen appliances for the aspiring chef and home cook. www.sageappliances.co.uk

Franklins Farm Shop, London Farm shop with particular emphasis on artisan British products. www.franklinsrestaurant.com

Flock and Herd Butchery, London Specialising in locally sourced meat and game. www.flockandherd.com

Moxon's Fresh Fish, London Wide variety of British-sourced fish and seafood. Also freshly smoke their own fish. www.moxonsfreshfish.com

Atari-Ya Chain of Japanese shops in London. www.atariya.co.uk

Wing Thai Asian supermarket chain. Nationwide.

Wai Yee Hong Online Asian store. www.waiyeehong.com

Andreas, London A purveyor of fine fruit and veg. Delivers nationwide. www.andreasveg.co.uk

Panzers Deli and Grocery, London This wonderful store stocks a wide and varied array of American dry goods and foodstuffs as well as having a Jewish deli counter and bakery. www.panzers.co.uk

Hopleys Farm Shop, Bewdley, Worcestershire Selling everything from locally sourced fruit to craft beer. www.hopleysfarmshop.com

Mr Lawrence Wine Merchant, London Craft ale and wine specialist. Delivers nationwide. www.mrlawrencewinemerchant.co.uk

Neil's Yard Dairy cheeses of outstanding quality predominantly hailing from the British Isles. Delivers nationwide. www.nealsyarddairy.co.uk

Brick House Bakery, London Wonderful slow-fermented San Francisco-style bread. www.brickhousebread.com

Vadasz Deli, London Outstanding pickles, kimchi and sauerkraut using traditional cured ingredients. www.vadaszdeli.co.uk

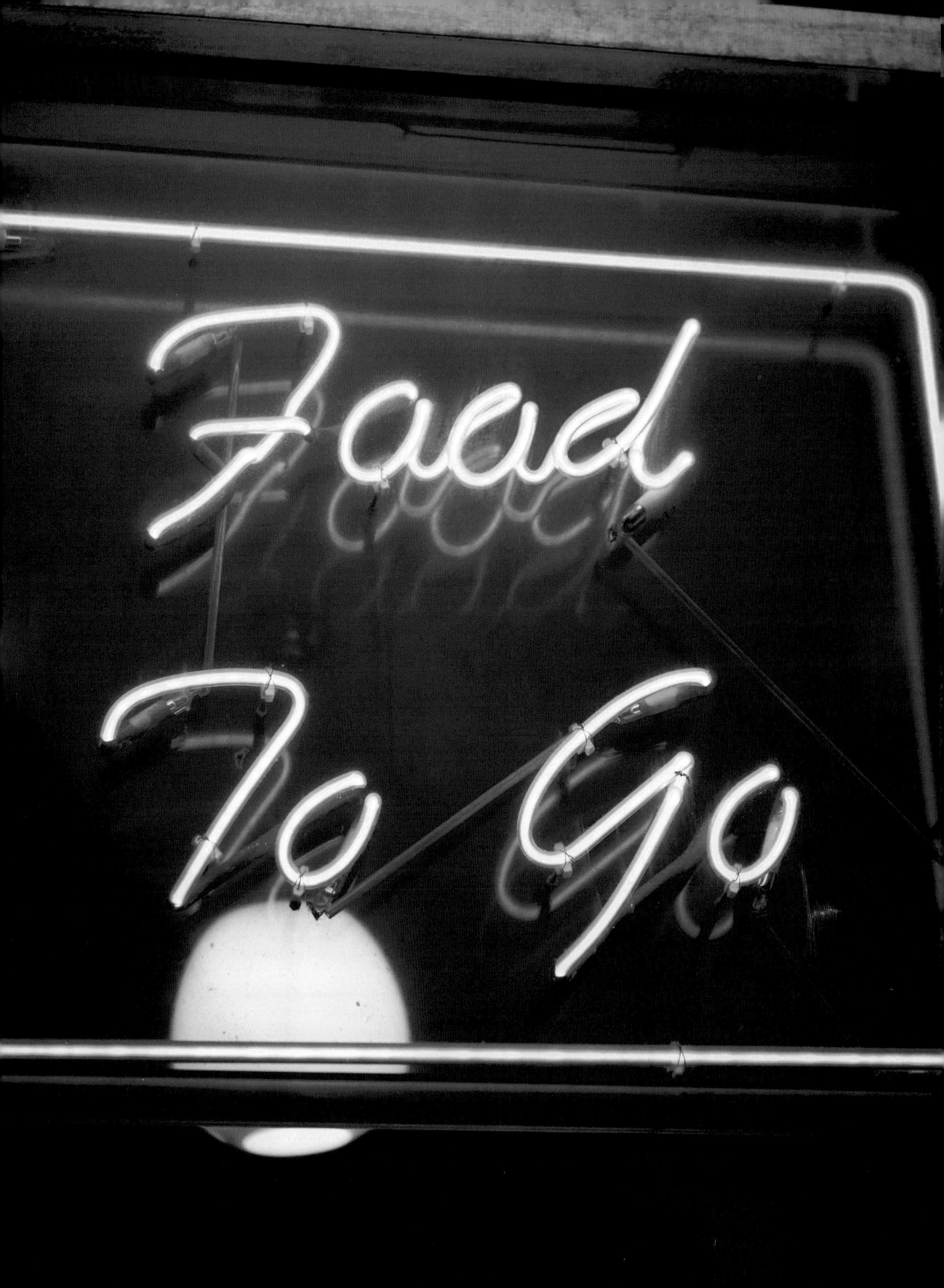
Food
To Go

Rules of the Fakeaway

Spoon measurements Unless the recipe is for something that is baked, these are heaped and are rough guides. For many dishes, you don't just want to pay lip service and slavishly follow a recipe no matter how it tastes. This isn't 'tourist food' – it's meant to stir the senses, so taste often and adjust things to suit your palate.

Charcoal should be dry lump wood and the best quality you can source. Lump wood will give you a lively, sustained cooking heat, and is quicker to light than chemically produced charcoals. Look for natural firelighters as they are usually odourless and chemical-free.

Salt is always flaky and from a natural source. It not only enhances dishes but in some cases also gives a wonderful texture. Add some at the start of cooking and it will help to draw out flavours.

Pepper is always freshly milled. For an interesting mix, look for Bristol five-blend pepper, which is a mixture of pink, black, green and white peppercorns and allspice berries.

Spices should be bought loose in specialist supermarkets or stores and ground yourself, where possible. Many spice-growing countries grade spices before they are sold on, and what ends up in the jars of ready-ground spices may not be the pick of the crop.

Flour I try to use (when available) stoneground flour, since this is thought to be more nutritionally sound than roller-milled flours. Stoneground flour is also said to have a better flavour as it contains both the germ and the bran. I personally think it makes more interesting cakes, breads and sauces, though it may lack the structure that roller-milled flour will give.

Yeast There are various types of yeast available. If you can get your hands on fresh yeast then you can use it interchangeably in the recipes – the process is still the same, just activate it in a little warm water with a pinch of sugar. You can use easy-blend (rapid-rise) yeast if you prefer (which doesn't need to be activated in warm water), but I personally don't think that this fast-action yeast gives you a better rise than active dried yeast.

Butter in my opinion should always be salty unless it's ghee or otherwise specified. A little pinch of salt is always good even in sweet dishes; salty butter does this for you!

Oil I try to use local oil such as rapeseed wherever possible, but groundnut (peanut) oil is excellent for shallow-frying. Reserve extra virgin olive oil or cold-pressed rapeseed oil for dressings and dips.

Eggs are always free-range and as fresh as possible.

Chicken and poultry is always free-range. Free-range birds should have a bit more chew in them and, dare I say it, may be a bit tougher than cage-reared ones, but this is worth it for the added flavour, not to mention the peace of mind. You can always pop it in a marinade to tenderise and impart flavour before cooking.

Fish really must be responsibly sourced and as fresh as possible. As a rule of thumb, try not to buy supermarket fish as it can be a lot older than you think it is. Speak to the local fish shop, ask where their produce comes from and don't be shy to press for an answer! Sometimes they will make a suggestion as to what's freshest or a good substitute, or tell you about something seasonal that is a rare treat. Buy fish and cook it on the same day where possible.

Meat When buying meat there are a few considerations to make. Avoid any that is packaged as 'stewing', 'frying' or 'minced' (ground) as this often consists of mixed cuts, which may not be suitable and can cook at different times and temperatures. Instead, try to go to a butcher. Any good one should be able to tell you the origin of its produce. Look for outdoor-reared meat and avoid grain-fed meat.

Fruit and veg should be the freshest you can get your hands on. Try to follow the seasons, when the food is more plentiful, much cheaper and, most importantly, at its tastiest! Look out for farmers' markets – they are a great source of locally produced food that usually tastes amazing.

Lemons and limes Buy unwaxed! No exceptions.

to a simmer and leave to bubble away for about 45 minutes. Strain through a sieve and cool down as quickly as possible. You can skim off any fat that forms on the surface as it cools, then freeze it in small batches so you have lovely stock on hand whenever you need it. Your local butcher will usually give away bones for stock, too, so it's worth asking.

• Always make sure you have ice cubes in the freezer, as they are a great way of rapidly cooling water that can be used to speedily refresh blanched vegetables or fruits, which will help them retain their colour and texture. Iced water can also be used for chilling hard-boiled eggs before you peel them (peel them while they are still a little warm though, as it's much easier to get their shells off that way).

• Avoid refrigerating chillies, as they tend to spoil rapidly because of the condensation of the fridge. They keep very well in a fruit or citrus bowl, or can be frozen.

• Remove large joints of meat from the fridge about 30 minutes before cooking so they come up to room temperature. This will help maintain the cooking temperature of the oven or barbecue, though do use your discretion on warm days.

• A lot of the recipes in this book (especially when large cuts of meat are concerned) can be cooked either over a barbecue or in a low and slow oven. I tend to slow-cook at about 110ºC/230ºf/Gas ¼, which sounds very low. However, this ensures your meat cooks while it is in a relaxed state, whereas cooking at an intense heat causes it to cook in a perplexed state, often bowing and altering its shape.

• Do yourself a favour and make up batches of minced ginger and garlic in a food processor, which you can then freeze in mini ice cube trays so they are ready to use. These can be dropped into a hot pan, will thaw in seconds, and pack a powerful flavour punch.

• Use a damp sheet of kitchen paper or a dish cloth to fix your chopping board in place so it doesn't move around while you are chopping.

• Don't keep tomatoes or eggs in the fridge – it's too cold for the tomatoes and will mean their flavour and texture will suffer, and eggs are porous and tend to absorb the flavours from other foods in your fridge. What's more, when you use eggs for baking you want them at room temperature.

• When slicing onions, two things can help avoid tears: a sharp knife, which cuts through the tiny plant cells without crushing them, and breathing through your open mouth. There are a million more tips, too, though many are apocryphal.

• You may notice I use a lot of fresh root ginger. A quick, easy and painless way to peel it is to use a teaspoon and scrape the skin off. No more fiddly peeling or waste.

• You may also notice that I use a lot of garlic. Buy a good crusher, which will mince your garlic and should be fairly easy to clean. To peel garlic in a hurry, trim off the woody tops with the tip of a knife, then, using the widest part of a knife, squash the garlic into the board. They should slip their skins easily.

• A low oven (110ºC/230ºf/Gas ¼) can be used for keeping food warm once it has been cooked while you finish off something else, as well as for sterilising jars. To do the latter, wash the jars and lids scrupulously with hot water and plenty of soap, then rinse and drip dry. Invert the jars and leave them to bake (of sorts) for about 15 minutes. Try not to handle them internally. Place hot liquid into the jar and seal tightly.

• A roast chicken carcass or other bones makes a great stock. Simply chuck the stripped carcass (or carcasses, if you've saved some up in the freezer) into cold water, bring

文
家口酒
興

歡
外迎
賣

TAKE AWAY WELCOME

ท่านสามารถสั่งกลับบ้านได้
ขอบพระคุณค่ะ

The Recipes

Multigrain porridge

DIFFICULTY RATING:

SPECIAL EQUIPMENT:
Thermal vacuum flask

SERVES: 4

PREP TIME: 5 minutes, plus
overnight soaking (optional)

COOKING TIME:
12–20 minutes

For a make-ahead on-the-go breakfast, this recipe can be packed into a thermal vacuum flask, where it will stay warm, fresh flavoured and yielding in texture for up to 12 hours. Depending on how you feel, you can go for a protein-rich porridge with the addition of nuts and seeds, an indulgent porridge with whole milk and honey, or a more savoury porridge with a little more salt. Here, the oats are toasted before being simmered, which gives them a nutty finish. If you like the texture of your porridge smooth use quick-cook oats, if slightly coarse, use whole or jumbo rolled oats.

If you have time to soak the oats overnight it will cut down the final cooking time by about 10 minutes.

175g/6oz/2 cups jumbo oats
300ml/½ pint/1¼ cups cold water
400ml/14fl oz/1⅔ cups milk (cow's, nut, soya, oat – whichever you prefer)
105ml/5 tbsp buckwheat flakes
pinch of salt
splash of pouring cream (optional)

TO SERVE

spoonful each of sunflower seeds and golden linseeds
generous handful of blueberries
handful of roasted hazelnuts, roughly chopped
trickle of good-quality honey, to serve

1 Lightly toast the oats in a dry frying pan over a medium heat for 2–3 minutes, until fragrant. Tip them into a bowl. If you plan to soak the oats overnight, add the water and milk now, stir, and place in the fridge.

2 Using the same frying pan, lightly toast the sunflower seeds and linseeds for 2–3 minutes, until fragrant. Set aside.

3 Put the soaked oats, or the toasted oats, water and milk, along with the buckwheat flakes and salt into a large pan over a medium heat.

4 Bring to a gentle simmer and cook for 5 minutes, stirring regularly. Place a lid on the pan and remove from the heat. Allow the grains to swell for 5 minutes, adding a little more water, milk – or pouring cream if you're feeling indulgent – if it's too thick.

5 Spoon the porridge into a preheated flask or four bowls.

6 When ready to serve, top each portion with seeds, blueberries, hazelnuts and honey.

Sausage, egg & muffin sandwich

DIFFICULTY:

SPECIAL EQUIPMENT:
2 cooking rings; 8cm/3½in
pastry cutter; heavy griddle

SERVES: 4

PREP TIME: 30 minutes,
plus 1½ hours proving

COOKING TIME: 30 minutes

400g/14oz good-quality pork sausage
meat (bulk sausage)

oil, for cooking

4 eggs

4 x 25g/1oz slices red
Leicester cheese

Home-made Ketchup (see page 131),
to serve

FOR THE MUFFINS

10g/¼oz easy-blend (rapid rise)
dried yeast

5ml/1 tsp sugar

275ml/9fl oz/1¼ cups milk

400g/14oz/3½ cups strong
white bread flour

pinch of salt

oil or melted butter, for greasing
and cooking

coarse cornmeal, for sprinkling

An indulgence enjoyed at a certain burger chain by people around the world, this is the ultimate comfort food and is well worth mastering at home for a leisurely Sunday morning brunch. In this version, high-quality pork is formed into succulent patties and fried before being encased in a fluffy home-made muffin and topped with a fried egg – hangover heaven. This recipe makes eight muffins, so you can keep the ones you don't use in the freezer, ready to whip out and toast whenever the craving takes you. They are also perfect for another breakfast treat: eggs Benedict.

1 Activate the yeast by putting it in a bowl with the sugar and a tablespoon of the milk and stirring together briefly. Set aside in a warm place and leave it for 5–10 minutes, until the surface is frothy.

2 Sift the flour and salt into a large bowl. Make a well in the centre and add the rest of the milk. Add the frothy yeast mixture and mix to form a soft, sticky dough.

3 Turn out the dough on to a floured surface and knead it for 8–10 minutes, until smooth and elastic. Grease the inside of the bowl, add the dough, cover with clear film (plastic wrap) and leave in a warm place for about an hour, until doubled in size.

4 Using your fist, knock back (punch down) the dough, then tip it on to a lightly floured surface. Roll it out to a rectangle about 1.5cm/¾in thick and use a lightly floured plain 8cm/3½in cutter to cut out eight rounds, reshape any excess trimmings.

5 Dust a medium baking tray with a little cornmeal. Place the muffins on the tray, cover loosely with a clean dish towel and leave in a warm place for 25–30 minutes to prove, until nearly doubled in size.

6 Preheat the oven to 180ºC/350ºF/ Gas 4, and put a heavy griddle pan over a medium heat. With a piece of kitchen towel wipe a little oil or melted butter over the surface of the pan. Sprinkle a little cornmeal on to the tops of the risen muffins.

7 Carefully cook the muffins on the hot griddle in batches of three or four for about 8–10 minutes on each side, until golden brown. If you have another pan and can manage it, you could cook two batches at once to save time.

8 Transfer the muffins to the baking tray and bake in the oven for another 5 minutes to cook through. Once cooked, put the muffins on a wire rack to cool.

9 When you are ready to cook, divide the sausage meat into four equal portions and shape into balls. Set out the cooking rings and put a ball in each, then squash them down into flat patties using the back of a spoon. Lift off the rings and wash, ready to be used for the eggs.

10 Put a little oil in a frying pan and set it over a medium-high heat. Add the patties and fry for 4–5 minutes on each side, until golden. Set aside and keep warm. Reduce the heat to medium.

11 Grease the inside of the cooking rings with a little oil, then put them in the frying pan. Pour 2.5ml/½ tsp oil into each ring, then crack an egg into each one. Cook for 3–4 minutes or to your liking. Remove and place on top of the warmed sausage patty.

12 Split four muffins in half and toast the insides in the frying pan. Place the bottom slice on a plate, add the patty, the cheese and the egg, and finally the top layer of the muffin. Serve immediately with ketchup.

COOK'S TIP
You could try adding different flavourings, seasoning and spices to the sausage meat, such as mixed herbs and grated onion, or garlic, fresh chilli and cracked black pepper.

Avocado on toast with soft egg

DIFFICULTY :

EQUIPMENT: N/a

SERVES: 4

PREP TIME: 5-10 minutes

COOKING TIME: 10 minutes

The hugely popular avocado on toast is a great way to take in exceptional levels of monunosaturated (good) fats, the same levels of potassium as a banana and more fibre than an apple. It's also a doddle to make at home. You could make your own sourdough – although this is a lengthy process that involves creating (and then feeding regularly, like a pet) a mother or starter culture from bread and water and then using a little of this to create your bread – or you can just buy a decent loaf. As a rule of thumb, a loaf of real sourdough should cost the same as a pint of beer (the brewing process being similar to the bread-making process). The runny egg yolk gives the avocado a rich coating, and a spicy sauce adds pep.

4 eggs

45ml/3 tbsp avocado oil or olive oil

4 slices sourdough bread, sliced lengthways

2 medium ripe avocados

salt and ground black pepper, to taste

shichimi togarashi or any spicy sauce, to serve

1 Bring a medium pan of generously salted water to a rolling boil. Lower in the eggs gently and cook for 5 minutes. Remove with a slotted spoon and place in a bowl of cold water until just warm, then peel and set aside.

2 Preheat a griddle pan over a medium heat. Drizzle a little oil on each side of the bread, then griddle it for 2–3 minutes on each side, until golden and crispy. Set aside on a warmed plate.

3 Slice the avocados lengthways and twist to separate the two halves. Using a tablespoon, take out and discard the stone, then scoop out the flesh and put it into a bowl. Mash with a fork to give you a rough texture, then season to taste.

4 Spread equal portions of the mashed avocado over the toast, then top each with an egg and slice it in two or pierce the white so the yolk can run over the avocado, giving you a rich and delicious sauce.

5 Serve the toasts immediately with shichimi togarashi or your spicy sauce of choice.

COOK'S TIP
Shichimi togarashi is a condiment made from a mixture of chillies, sesame seeds, seaweed and ginger, to name but a few of the ingredients. You can buy it in some supermarkets' Japanese sections or online.

Edamame bean salad

Simple to make, simple to pop in your mouth – this recipe uses edamame beans in their pods, which are available frozen in supermarkets, so there are no excuses for not making this! It is usually served as an afterthought from your local takeaway and cold to boot, but here we have warmed through the vibrant green beans in a wok and seasoned them with fiery chillies and sesame oil to create a really exciting snack or accompaniment.

DIFFICULTY: 🥄
EQUIPMENT: Wok with a lid
SERVES: 2
PREP TIME: 5 minutes
COOKING TIME: 3-4 minutes

5ml/1 tsp sesame oil

300g/11oz fresh or frozen edamame beans in their pods

30ml/2 tbsp gochujang chilli paste

1 fresh red chilli, seeded and chopped

30ml/2 tbsp black and white sesame seeds, toasted

pinch of salt

1 Pour the oil into a wok and place over a medium heat.

2 Add the edamame beans to the wok, along with a good splash of water if you are using fresh ones – this will help to steam the pods.

3 Put the lid on the wok and steam the beans for 3–4 minutes, until just tender.

4 Remove the lid and stir in the gochujang, chilli and sesame seeds. Sprinkle over the salt and serve warm in little bowls.

Popcorn chicken

DIFFICULTY: 🍳🍳

EQUIPMENT: Deep-fryer or a large, heavy pan suitable for deep-frying

SERVES: 4-6

PREP TIME: 10 minutes, plus 1 hour marinating

COOKING TIME: 8-12 minutes

4 medium chicken breasts, skinned and cut into bite-sized chunks

280ml/9fl oz/generous 1 cup buttermilk

vegetable oil, for deep-frying

190g/6 oz/1²/₃ cups tapioca flour

2.5ml/¹/₂ tsp each of cayenne pepper, garlic powder and onion powder

salt and ground black pepper

Barbecue Sauce (see page 64), and/or Home-made Ketchup (see page 131) and/or Hot Sauce (see page 130), to serve

Crisp fried chicken, with its succulent interior and golden jacket, is a favourite takeaway or meal-on-the-run choice all over the world, but suffers from a bad reputation. Using free-range, high-welfare chicken breast, however, and fresh spices makes it a top-quality snack. It's also very quick and easy to make at home. The 'popcorn' part of this recipe's name refers to the texture of the chicken, which is soaked into succulence in some buttermilk and then coated in tapioca flour before being plunged briefly into hot oil. The resulting golden nuggets cry out to be dipped into piquant sauces.

1 Put the chicken chunks into a bowl, pour over the buttermilk, stir to coat, and leave to marinate for at least 1 hour in the fridge.

2 When you're ready to cook, heat the oil to 180°C/350°F in a deep-fryer or large, heavy pan suitable for deep-frying. Test whether it is ready by putting a piece of bread in the oil. If it spits and fizzes, the oil is ready.

3 Meanwhile, mix together the flour, cayenne pepper, garlic and onion powders and salt and pepper in a shallow dish.

4 Lift the chicken pieces from the buttermilk and dredge through the flour mixture. Allow the flour to gather around the chicken – it's OK if the surface has a rough texture.

5 Carefully lower the coated chicken into the hot oil and cook for 4–5 minutes, until golden and crispy. You'll need to work in batches to avoid overcrowding the pan. Once cooked, remove to a plate lined with kitchen paper to drain while you cook the remaining chicken.

6 Serve immediately with whichever sauce(s) you like best.

Sesame prawn toasts

DIFFICULTY:

EQUIPMENT: Mortar and pestle, food processor

SERVES: 4-6

PREP TIME: 15 minutes

COOKING TIME: 25-30 minutes

200g/7oz raw prawns (shrimp), peeled and deveined

3 spring onions (scallions), finely sliced

5ml/1 tsp Sichuan peppercorns, finely crushed

30ml/2 tbsp cornflour (cornstarch)

1 egg, lightly beaten

15ml/1 tbsp sesame oil

15ml/1 tbsp light soy sauce

4 slices of day-old bread, crusts removed, cut into triangles

60ml/4 tbsp mixed black and white sesame seeds

150ml/¼ pint/⅔ cup oil, for frying

cucumber wedges sprinkled with salt and rice wine vinegar, to serve (optional)

FOR THE SWEET CHILLI DIPPING SAUCE:

175ml/6fl oz/¾ cup Chinese rice vinegar

15ml/1 tbsp fish sauce

90g/3½oz/½ cup caster (superfine) sugar

pinch of salt

8 Serrano chillies, seeded and chopped

1 garlic clove, peeled and roughly chopped

4cm/1½in piece of fresh root ginger, roughly chopped

lime juice, to taste

These retro faves are a guilty pleasure of many a takeaway order, but making your own is both tasty and rewarding and won't be jammed full of MSG. They are usually eaten as a snack or starter and can be made ahead of time and chilled until you're ready to cook them. They are served with a sweet chilli dipping sauce, which can also be prepared in advance and stored in an airtight jar in the fridge.

1 To make the sweet chilli dipping sauce, put the vinegar, fish sauce, sugar and salt in a small pan and stir over a gentle heat until the sugar has dissolved. Bring up to a simmer and simmer for 12–15 minutes, until the mixture forms a thick syrup.

2 Meanwhile, bash together the chillies, garlic and ginger with a mortar and pestle or in a food processor until they form a paste. Add this to the syrup along with the lime juice and cook for 1–2 minutes. Pour into a sterilised jar (see page xx) and set aside to cool. Seal and store in the fridge.

3 To make the prawn toasts, put the prawns, spring onions, pepper, cornflour, egg, sesame oil and soy sauce in a food processor. Pulse the mixture until it forms a thick paste. You could also do this with a heavy knife and a chopping board.

4 Spread a heaped tablespoon of the mixture to the edges of the bread. Sprinkle with sesame seeds to cover the surface (the paste should act like a good glue).

5 Heat 45ml/3 tbsp of the oil in a large frying pan over a medium heat. Add the bread triangles and shallow-fry for 3–4 minutes, until the bread is golden and crisp. You may need to do this in batches – try not to overcrowd the pan as you'll need space to turn the toasts. Turn and cook on the sesame side for a couple of minutes.

6 Drain on a plate lined with kitchen paper. Keep warm and serve with chilli sauce and some cucumber wedges sprinkled with salt and rice wine vinegar, if you like.

COOK'S TIP

Sichuan pepper is one of the key ingredients in Chinese five-spice, and brings a lemony note to the party. It is available in supermarkets and Chinese stores.

Tandoori prawns

DIFFICULTY :

EQUIPMENT: 4 long metal skewers

SERVES: 4

PREP TIME: 5 minutes, plus 1 hour marinating

COOKING TIME: 6–8 minutes

This curry-house classic is traditionally cooked in a clay oven or tandoor on a long skewer, but you can come close to replicating the blistering temperatures using a grill or broiler, a barbecue with a lid or, if you happen to have one, a ceramic barbecue or a wood-fired pizza oven. The choice of fuel is important: usually in India a tandoor will use lump wood charcoal but good, dry, seasoned wood is also suitable. The fuel should be smouldering rather than raging flames.

The prawns are also important and should be shell-on but deveined. The bigger the prawns the better so they can withstand the high temperatures of the barbecue and take on a nice, golden, flavoursome charred exterior, yet still remain moist inside.

1kg/2 lb raw king prawns (jumbo shrimp), shell-on but deveined

15ml/1 tbsp vegetable oil

2 lemons, cut into quarters, for keeping the prawns on the skewers

lime or lemon wedges, to serve

Indian Chutneys (see page 132) and Naan (see page 129), to serve

FOR THE MARINADE

75ml/5 tbsp natural (plain) yogurt

pinch each of salt and ground black pepper

5ml/1 tsp finely chopped fresh green chillies

2 garlic cloves, peeled and finely crushed

5cm/2in piece of fresh root ginger, peeled and finely grated

pinch of ground turmeric

5ml/1 tsp garam masala

juice of 1 lime

small bunch of curry leaves, chopped

1 Mix the marinade ingredients together in a large bowl. Add the prawns and mix it all up with your hands so the marinade coats the prawns. Set aside for about an hour.

2 Preheat the barbecue, grill (broiler) or wood-fired oven.

3 When you are ready to get cooking, thread the prawns on to the metal skewers. Place half a lemon on the end of each skewer to stop the prawns sliding off.

4 Lay the skewers flat on the barbecue or under the grill or, if possible, standing upright – as they would be cooked in a tandoor. Cook for 3–4 minutes on each side.

5 Remove from the skewers and serve with lemon or lime wedges, Indian Chutneys and Naan.

Vietnamese vegetable rolls

DIFFICULTY: 🍳

EQUIPMENT: N/a

SERVES: 4

PREP TIME: 25 minutes

COOKING TIME: N/A

The cuisine of Vietnam is a cultural blend of the finesse of French classical food and some of the delicate herbs and spices from China and India. These crunchy, flavoursome yet light rice paper rolls showcase this heritage, and once you have everything ready to roll are quick and simple to assemble. Simply rehydrate the wrappers until they become pliable and swiftly fill with your favourite fish, meats and vegetables before they become too soft. Using holy basil will totally transform the filling by bringing a pronounced warming note of aniseed, giving your dish real authenticity.

50g/2oz fine rice noodles

bunch of fresh holy basil, leaves only

bunch of fresh mint, leaves only

small bunch of fresh coriander (cilantro), leaves only

handful of long chives

1 Little Gem (Bibb) lettuce, finely shredded

3 medium carrots, peeled and finely shredded into matchsticks 12 medium cooked prawns (shrimp), peeled and halved lengthways

½ cucumber, peeled, seeded and sliced into fine matchsticks

3 spring onions (scallions), trimmed and thinly sliced lengthways

2 fresh red chillies, seeded and sliced

50g/2oz/¼ cup bean sprouts

12 rice paper wrappers

FOR THE DIPPING SAUCE

juice of 1 lime

15ml/1 tbsp Thai fish sauce

45ml/3 tbsp dark soy sauce

2 garlic cloves, peeled and crushed

30ml/2 tbsp chilli sauce

5ml/1 tsp grated palm sugar or soft light brown sugar

1 Soak the noodles in boiling water for 15 minutes, or according to the packet instructions. Drain and set aside.

2 Meanwhile, make the dipping sauce by combining all the ingredients and putting them in a dipping bowl.

3 Prepare all the other ingredients, apart from the wrappers – once you start making the rolls you will need everything ready and to hand.

4 Fill a large bowl with a little warm water. Softening and then filling just one at a time, dip a rice paper wrapper in the water for about 10 seconds, until pliable and softened around the edges. Place on a board and immediately lay a few of each of the fresh herb leaves and a couple of long chives along the centre of the wrapper. Top with some of the lettuce, noodles and carrots, three of the prawns, and then the cucumber, spring onion, chillies and bean sprouts. Try to ensure that the ingredients all go the same way and leave a rim of about 5cm/2in around the filling mound.

5 Sprinkle a couple more herb leaves on top, roll one edge inwards to cover the filling and then tightly roll up the wrapper to form a cigar shape.

6 Lay the finished roll on a tray seam side down so it binds and repeat with the remaining wrappers.

7 Serve the rolls immediately with the dipping sauce.

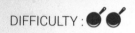

DIFFICULTY :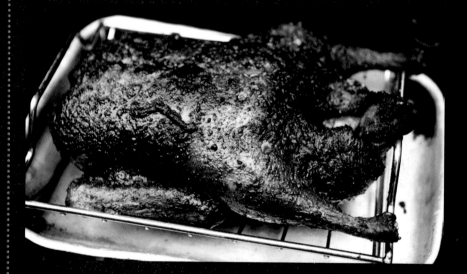

EQUIPMENT: Roasting rack, and deep roasting tray

SERVES: 4-6

PREP TIME: 10-15 minutes, plus 24 hours marinating

COOKING TIME: about 1½ hours

Peking duck is a real staple on menus at Chinese restaurants and takeaways worldwide. The key to that crispy skin is to get rid of as much moisture as possible. In a domestic kitchen the best way to do this is to buzz the skin with a warm hairdryer to drive off any excess moisture, after the duck has been marinated in a rub for 24 hours to draw out the moisture. The true advantages of home-made over takeaway Peking duck is that it is genuinely easy to cook, you can find a really delicious duck from a local source, the vegetables can be fresh, moist and crispy, and the home-made hoisin sauce takes the dish to a whole new flavour level.

1.6–1.8kg/3½–4lb duck (see Cook's Tip)

7.5ml/1½ tsp Chinese five-spice powder

5ml/1 tsp ground ginger

2.5ml/½ tsp ground black pepper

15ml/1 tbsp salt

15ml/1 tbsp soy sauce

60ml/4 tbsp Shaoxing wine

5ml/1 tsp liquid smoke

FOR THE HOISIN SAUCE

500g/1¼lb ripe plums, halved and stoned

15ml/1 tbsp Chinese five-spice powder

45ml/3 tbsp soft dark brown sugar

30ml/2 tbsp light soy sauce

2.5ml/½ tsp ground black pepper

10ml/2 tsp sesame oil

TO SERVE

12 Chinese pancakes, warmed according to the instructions

½ cucumber, sliced lengthways into thin matchsticks

spring onions (scallions), trimmed and thinly sliced lengthways

Remove all the packaging from the duck and anything from inside the cavity. Remove any excess skin and fat from the neck end. Place the duck in a container that has a lid.

Combine the Chinese five-spice powder, ground ginger, pepper, salt, soy sauce, Shaoxing wine and liquid smoke in a bowl, then rub all over the skin and inside the cavity of the duck.

Place the duck breast side up in the fridge and leave it, with the lid on, for up to 12 hours. Rub any of the seasoning that has gathered in the bottom of the tray on to the breasts,

then turn it over so it is breast side down. Leave for a further 12 hours.

Remove the duck from the fridge about an hour before cooking to bring it up to room temperature. Use a hair dryer to dry the skin all over but especially on the top.

Preheat the oven to 200ºC/400ºF/ Gas 6. Using a large needle or metal skewer, pierce the duck deeply around the breasts and thighs. Put the duck on a roasting rack inside a deep roasting tray. Roast in the centre of the oven for about 1½ hours.

When the leg meat starts to come away from the bone the meat is cooked. If the skin is still not crispy, turn the oven up to 220ºC/425ºF/Gas 7 and cook for a further 10–15 minutes. Remove from the oven and rest.

While the bird is cooking, make the hoisin sauce by putting all the ingredients into a medium pan and simmering until smooth and pulpy. Pass through a sieve and place in a serving bowl.

When ready to serve, slice off the legs from the duck and, using two forks, shred or pull the meat from these and the main body of the duck. Mix the shredded meat with the crispy skin and set aside on a warmed plate.

To serve, smear the base of a warm pancake with a teaspoon of sauce, add a generous amount of duck and top with cucumber and spring onions. Roll up and eat.

COOK'S TIPS
- If you come across 'Pekin' duck, this is not a spelling mistake but the breed of duck that is used traditionally for the dish. I recommend using Gressingham duck, which is a cross between a wild mallard and a Pekin.
- Chinese pancakes are available in most supermarkets or online. They can be warmed on a low setting in a microwave or in a steaming basket.
- Although hoisin sauces are available in most supermarkets and Asian stores it is worth having a go at making your own, especially during plum season when they're cheap and plentiful. Try experimenting with different plums, such as mirabelles or damsons.

Pork and prawn gyoza

DIFFICULTY : 🥄🥄

EQUIPMENT: Large frying pan with a tight-fitting lid

MAKES: About 20

PREP TIME: 10–15 minutes

COOKING TIME: 6–8 minutes per batch

Dumplings come in many forms and appear in many cuisines, but it's believed the Chinese version is the oldest, dating back 1,800 years. Much like ravioli, these gyoza have a frilly folded edge – but it's their crispy bases that make them so special, and has earned them the name 'pot stickers'. This is a really versatile recipe that allows you to use a variety of fillings, and they can be made ahead of time and cooked for big numbers in a large pan with a lid. Gyoza are at their best eaten straight from the pan, when you will be able to appreciate the caramelised crunchy bases. It takes a while to make them but after the first 10 or so you'll be an expert!

20 gyoza skins

30ml/2 tbsp oil, for frying

FOR THE FILLING

100g/3¾oz raw prawns (shrimp), peeled, deveined and finely chopped

200g/7oz minced (ground) pork

5ml/1 tsp cornflour (cornstarch)

225g/8oz canned water chestnuts, drained and finely chopped

75g/3oz fresh shiitake mushrooms, finely chopped

45ml/3 tbsp light soy sauce

15ml/1 tbsp sesame oil

5ml/1 tsp mirin

2 spring onions (scallions), trimmed and finely sliced

½ sweetheart cabbage, trimmed and finely chopped

2 garlic cloves, peeled and crushed

2.5cm/1in piece of fresh root ginger, peeled and grated

plenty of ground black pepper

FOR THE DIPPING SAUCE

30ml/2 tbsp rice vinegar

30ml/2 tbsp dark soy sauce

5ml/1 tsp Japanese chilli oil (La-Yu)

1 spring onion (scallion), trimmed and finely sliced

1 Prepare the filling by mixing all the ingredients together in a medium bowl, until thoroughly combined.

2 Lay the gyoza skins flat on a surface and spoon a teaspoon of the mixture into the centre of each. Moisten the edges with a little cold water and then fold over to create a half-moon shape. Pinch with your fingers to create a frilly edge.

3 When all the dumplings are made, heat the oil in a large frying pan (with a lid) over a medium heat.

4 Place the gyoza flat side down in the hot oil; you can cook 10–15 at a time. Cook for 2–3 minutes, until a golden caramelised crust has formed on the base.

5 Stand back and pour about 100ml/3½fl oz/scant ½ cup of water into the pan – it will sizzle and spit a little. When it dies down, put the lid on and allow the gyoza to steam for 4–5 minutes, until the filling is cooked and the gyoza appear slightly translucent. Remove to a plate and keep warm while you cook the remaining gyoza in the same way.

6 To make the dipping sauce, combine all the ingredients in a bowl. Serve with the warm gyoza.

COOK'S TIPS

• Freeze the prepared raw gyoza by laying them spaced well apart on a plastic tray lined with baking parchment for 3–4 hours. Remove them from the tray and place them gently into zip-lock bags to be stashed away in the freezer.

• It might seem laborious to finely chop all the ingredients by hand instead of in a food processor, but the all-important texture should not feel too smooth and mousse-like.

Lamb samosas

DIFFICULTY: 🍳🍳

EQUIPMENT: Deep-fryer or large, heavy pan suitable for deep-frying

SERVES: 6

PREP TIME: 15–20 minutes

COOKING TIME: 25-30 minutes

Samosas come in a variety of forms up and down India — proper Punjabi ones tend to have a dense, almost bread-like pastry, whereas towards the south the pastry is shorter and crisper. Usually washed down with a cup of super-sweet, fragrant masala chai they are deep-fried in wok-like korai pans and served piping hot, unlike the flabby, greasy ready-made or takeaway ones you can buy elsewhere — it's definitely well worth making your own. Traditionally, mutton would be used but here we use lamb. Fresh green chillies are a must, though, and you should stand firm on this as they have a freshness and acidity that red chillies simply don't possess. If you can't get fresh curry leaves then dried will do.

FOR THE FILLING

15ml/1 tbsp oil

2 red onions, peeled and finely chopped

3 garlic cloves, peeled and crushed

thumb-sized piece of fresh root ginger, peeled and roughly chopped

2 small fresh green chillies, finely sliced

350g/12oz lean good-quality minced (ground) lamb

small bunch of fresh curry leaves, roughly chopped

pinch each of salt and ground turmeric

5ml/1 tsp garam masala

5ml/1 tsp cumin seeds, crushed

150g/5oz frozen peas, thawed

30ml/2 tbsp mango chutney

1 pack of samosa pastry (sometimes called 'samosa pads')

1 egg, lightly beaten

oil, for deep-frying

Mango Lassi, to serve (see page 148)

Sweet Tamarind Chutney, to serve (see page 132)

1 To make the filling, heat the oil in a large frying pan over a medium heat. Add the onion and cook for about 10 minutes, until sweet smelling and softened.

2 Add the garlic, ginger and chillies to the onions and cook for a couple of minutes, until softened.

3 Add the lamb to the pan and brown for about 5 minutes, stirring regularly, then stir in the remaining filling ingredients. Turn off the heat and set aside to cool.

4 Remove the samosa pastry from its packaging and lay out the 'pads' on a lightly floured surface.

5 Put a teaspoon of the filling into the bottom of the pocket of each pad. Seal the top of the cone and fold the triangles inwards. Brush around the edge with a little beaten egg and press to seal the edges really well.

6 Set aside and repeat until you've used up all the filling mixture.

7 When you're ready to cook the samosas, preheat the oil to about 180°C/350°F in a deep-fat fryer or suitable large, heavy pan. Test the temperature by dropping a piece of bread in the oil. If it spits and fizzes, the oil is ready.

8 In batches of four, deep-fry the samosas for 4–5 minutes, until a crisp golden brown. A lot of deep-fried food floats when it's cooked, and this applies here too.

9 Drain on kitchen paper and serve with a glass of Lassi and Sweet Tamarind Chutney.

COOK'S TIPS

• Ready-made samosa pastry can be bought frozen in the Indian section in supermarkets or speciality stores.

• If you want to freeze the samosas so you have a stash ready to go, place them raw and filled on baking parchment on a tray and open-freeze them before putting them in a zip-lock bag until required. They will need to be defrosted for about 90 minutes at room temperature before they can be cooked.

Korean salt, chilli & lime squid

This authentic Korean street food favourite is a delightful, crisp-and-crunchy, citrus-sharp classic that is dead easy to whip up at home. Look for baby squid in your local fishmonger or Asian supermarket, or you can use frozen ones. Ask the fishmonger to clean them for you by removing the quill and ink sack.

Although the size of the squid will affect how tender it is – smaller ones are preferable – there are a couple of things you can do to make it even more unctuous. Making cross-hatch incisions on the flesh before frying helps keep it tender, and cooking it in batches, very quickly in sizzling hot oil, means it doesn't have a chance to become rubbery and tough.

DIFFICULTY:

EQUIPMENT: Deep-fryer or a large, heavy pan suitable for deep-frying

SERVES: 2

PREP TIME: 10 minutes

COOKING TIME: 2–3 minutes

500g/1¼ lb baby squid, thawed if frozen
oil, for frying
2.5ml/½ tsp salt
2.5ml/½ tsp ground black pepper
1.5ml/¼ tsp garlic powder
1.5ml/¼ tsp onion powder
7.5ml/1½ tsp gochujang powder
150g/5oz/1¼ cups cornflour (cornstarch), sifted

FOR THE DIPPING SAUCE
45ml/3 tbsp light soy sauce
5ml/1 tsp sesame oil
5ml/1 tsp caster (superfine) sugar
5ml/1 tsp mirin
juice of 1 lime, or to taste

TO SERVE
lime wedges
2 fresh red chillies, seeded and finely sliced
2 spring onions (scallions), trimmed and finely sliced

1 Unless your fishmonger has done it for you, prepare the squid by washing them in plenty of cold clean water. Pat dry with kitchen paper. Place the tube with the open end facing you and run a very sharp knife from the bottom corner of the opening to the tip of the squid. Open it out and pat dry to remove any moisture. Using a blunt butter knife, gently make a cross-hatch pattern all over the surface.

2 Prepare the dipping sauce by mixing the soy sauce, sesame oil, sugar and mirin together in a small bowl. Stir until the sugar dissolves. Add lime juice to taste.

3 Heat the oil in a deep-fryer or large, deep pan suitable for deep-frying to 190°C/375°F.

4 Combine the salt, pepper, garlic, onion and gochujang powders and cornflour in a sbowl.

5 Take the prepared squid and dredge it through the cornflour mixture. Dust off any lumpy excess and carefully lower the squid into the hot oil. Cook for 2–3 minutes, until golden and crispy. You may need to work in batches.

6 Lift the cooked squid out with a slotted spoon and drain on a plate lined with kitchen paper.

7 Serve immediately with the dipping sauce, lime wedges and sliced fresh chillies and spring onions.

Thai style crab cakes

DIFFICULTY:

EQUIPMENT: Food processor or mortar and pestle, deep-fryer or large, heavy pan suitable for deep-frying

SERVES: 4

PREP TIME: 15 minutes

COOKING TIME:
12–16 minutes

3 fresh red chillies, seeded and roughly chopped

3 Thai shallots, peeled and roughly chopped

2 garlic cloves, peeled

1 lemongrass stalk, bruised with the back of a knife

1 thumb-sized piece of fresh root ginger, peeled and roughly chopped

1 thumb-sized piece of fresh galangal, peeled and roughly chopped

30ml/2 tbsp roughly chopped fresh coriander (cilantro), roots included

3 fresh kaffir lime leaves, stalks removed

400g/14oz mixed cooked crab meat, picked of any shell

1 egg, beaten

about 4 tbsp/60ml fresh breadcrumbs

Thai fish sauce, to taste

pinch each of salt and ground black pepper

oil, for deep-frying

Sweet Chilli Dipping Sauce (see page 33), to serve

Crab cakes that you find in Thai restaurants are generally made with crab meat that has been mixed together with cheaper cuts of fish, so they have less flavour and tend to be a bit rubbery. This recipe is the real deal and uses only crab meat to produce truly delicious, moist little cakes that cry out to be dunked in mouth-tingling home-made sweet chilli sauce. Brown and white crab meat are both used as, like yin and yang, the brown and the white balance each other to help give a rich and fresh seafood finish to the dish.

1 Blitz the chillies, shallots, garlic, lemongrass, ginger, galangal, coriander and kaffir lime leaves in a food processor or in a mortar with a pestle until it forms a paste.

2 Tip out the paste into a large bowl, then add the crab meat and combine to a smooth paste. Add the egg and breadcrumbs and combine. The mixture will stiffen slightly. If it is a little too wet then add some more breadcrumbs. Season with a little fish sauce and salt and pepper.

3 Divide the mixture into 20 small balls, then flatten them with the back of a spoon so they are about 1cm/½in thick by 5cm/2in across.

4 Heat the oil to 190°C/375°F in a deep-fryer or large, heavy pan suitable for deep-frying. Test a little spoonful of the mixture in the hot oil; if it starts to break up then stir in another tablespoon of breadcrumbs. Adjust the seasoning if necessary.

5 Deep-fry the cakes in small batches of five for 3–4 minutes, until crispy and golden.

6 Remove with a slotted spoon and drain on kitchen paper. Keep warm while you fry the remaining crab cakes.

7 Serve the crab cakes piping hot with sweet chilli dipping sauce.

COOK'S TIP
If you struggle to get fresh kaffir lime leaves then dried ones will do. If you do get hold of some fresh leaves then you can freeze the surplus in zip-lock bags.

Chicken satay

DIFFICULTY: 🍳

EQUIPMENT: Barbecue, 12 bamboo skewers

SERVES: 4

PREP TIME: 10 minutes, plus 2 hours marinating

COOKING TIME: 10-12 minutes

3 medium boneless, skinless chicken breasts

pickled cucumber and carrots, to serve (see Cook's Tip)

FOR THE MARINADE
2 garlic cloves, peeled and finely chopped

1 lemongrass stalk, very finely chopped

5ml/1 tsp ground ginger

5ml/1 tsp ground cumin

1.25ml/$\frac{1}{4}$ tsp ground turmeric

5ml/1 tsp ground coriander

45ml/3 tbsp flavourless oil

FOR THE PEANUT SAUCE
30ml/2 tbsp flavourless oil

4 Asian shallots, peeled and chopped

4 garlic cloves, peeled and crushed

1 lemongrass stalk, finely chopped

large piece of fresh root ginger, peeled and chopped

4 dried red chillies, soaked in water for 20 minutes, chopped

125g/4$\frac{1}{4}$oz/$\frac{2}{3}$ cup unsalted blanched peanuts, chopped

30ml/2 tbsp tamarind paste, mixed according to packet instructions

400ml/14fl oz can of coconut milk

soy sauce, to taste

Originating in Malaysia and Thailand, satays are usually strips of meat or fish that have been grilled over coals and are served with deep and flavourful sauces, in this case peanut. They are a firm favourite at street-food stands, served sizzling hot straight from the grill, but are less inspiring after sitting for a while in takeaway containers. Making your own gives you control over the quality of the meat and the spiciness of the sauce, as well as just tasting a million times better. There is more than enough sauce here, and it keeps well in a sealed container in the fridge for up to a week – try slathering it on grilled fish or vegetables.

1 Slice the chicken breasts lengthways into 2 x 10cm (3/4 x 4in) strips.

2 Prepare the marinade by mixing all the ingredients together in a large bowl. Add the chicken and stir to combine well. Cover and leave to sit for 2 hours in the fridge.

3 Meanwhile, soak the bamboo skewers in water, and preheat a barbecue to a medium heat, or set your grill to high.

4 To make the sauce, heat the oil in a heavy pan. Add the shallots, garlic, lemongrass and ginger and cook for 2–3 minutes to soften a little. Add the remaining ingredients and bring to a simmer for a couple of minutes.

5 Using a stick blender or food processor, blend to a smooth sauce; add a little water if it's too thick, and soy sauce to your taste.

6 Grill (broil) the meat over direct heat on the barbecue, or under a hot grill, for 3 minutes on each side, until cooked through and golden.

7 Serve immediately with pickled cucumber and carrots and the peanut dipping sauce.

COOK'S TIP
Make a quick cucumber pickle by thinly slicing a mini cucumber and tossing together with some matchstick carrots and beetroot. Dress with a pinch of salt, a pinch of sugar and a dash of rice wine vinegar.

Masala dosa

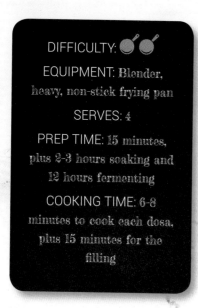

DIFFICULTY:

EQUIPMENT: Blender, heavy, non-stick frying pan

SERVES: 4

PREP TIME: 15 minutes, plus 2-3 hours soaking and 12 hours fermenting

COOKING TIME: 6-8 minutes to cook each dosa, plus 15 minutes for the filling

FOR THE DOSA BATTER

300g/11oz/1½ cups basmati rice
50g/2oz/¼ cup urad dhal
50g/2oz/¼ cup chana dhal
15ml/1 tbsp fenugreek seeds
pinch of salt
oil, for frying

FOR THE FILLING

500g/1¼lb waxy potatoes, chopped into 1cm/½in cubes
30ml/2 tbsp oil
2 red onions, finely chopped
15ml/1 tbsp black mustard seeds
30ml/2 tbsp urad dhal
30ml/2 tbsp chana dhal
2 dried chillies
3 fresh green chillies
handful of fresh curry leaves
5cm/2in-piece of fresh root ginger, peeled and grated
2.5ml/½ tsp ground turmeric
lemon juice, to taste
salt and ground black pepper

A dosa is a kind of pancake made from a fermented batter. This is a breakfast (or brunch) dish served throughout India but specifically in the south, where it is eaten in roadside vegetarian cafés and hotels. It is usually served with a spicy and sweet gravy and cooling coconut chutney – masala means 'spice mixture' in India. Suitable for vegans, this is a relatively simple dish to recreate, although you have to ferment the batter for 12–24 hours so you get that wonderful sour flavour and fluffy texture. The reward that you will get from making this yourself is a wonderfully crispy lace-like pancake that simply isn't possible with a takeaway.

1 The day before you want to eat the masala dosa, make the dosa batter by rinsing the rice in cold water until the water runs clear. Soak in a large bowl of fresh cold water for about 2–3 hours.

2 Rinse both types of dhal (lentils) and fenugreek seeds and soak them in more cold water in a separate bowl for 2–3 hours.

3 Drain the rice and lentils, reserving a little of the water. Liquidise the rice and lentils in a blender, adding some of the reserved soaking water if necessary, until you achieve a mixture with a grainy pouring consistency.

4 Cover and place in a large bowl in a warm draught-free area for about 12 hours or overnight to ferment and double in size. Warm weather will speed this up.

5 Once the batter is fermented and bubbly, heat a heavy non-stick frying pan over a medium heat and pour in 2.5ml/½ tsp oil. Put a couple of ladles of batter into the pan and sprinkle over a little salt, then swirl the batter around the pan. Cook for 3–4 minutes on each side, until crispy and golden. Set aside to keep warm and

repeat the process to make as many pancakes as you like. Any surplus mixture can be kept, covered, in the fridge for up to a week.

6 To make the filling, boil the potatoes in salted water for 8–10 minutes or until tender. Drain and break up slightly with a fork.

7 Meanwhile, put the oil into a large frying pan and place over a medium heat. Add the onions and cook for 10 minutes, until softened.

8 Add the mustards seeds and lentils and cook for 3–4 minutes. Stir in the dried and fresh chillies, curry leaves, ginger, turmeric, and salt, pepper and lemon juice to taste.

9 Combine the onion mixture with the broken-up potatoes and check the seasoning again, adjusting as necessary to taste.

10 Fill the warmed pancakes with the potato mixture, fold them over, and serve straight away.

Korean chicken wings

DIFFICULTY:

EQUIPMENT:
Barbecue with a lid

SERVES: 6

PREP TIME: 10 minutes,
plus time to prepare
the barbecue

COOKING TIME: 30 minutes

This recipe captures the backbone flavours of Korean cooking: garlic, ginger, chillies, spring onions and toasted sesame seeds. Barbecuing will help give your wings a charred and crispy finish. The best type of fuel to use is up for debate, but traditional Korean kitchens would use charcoal. The cooking method involves using direct heat for searing and colouring the wings, as well as indirect heat for finishing the cooking. Gochujang is a Korean red chilli paste made from fermented soybeans, chilli and rice flour that is available online. Look out for naturally fermented gochujang.

1.6kg/3½lb chicken wings

salt and ground black pepper

45ml/3 tbsp mixed sesame seeds, toasted

½ bunch of spring onions (scallions), green and white parts finely sliced, to serve

FOR THE HOT SAUCE

150g/5oz/generous ½ cup gochujang

45ml/3 tbsp mirin

75ml/5 tbsp light soy sauce

105ml/7 tbsp rice wine vinegar

thumb-sized piece of fresh root ginger, peeled and roughly chopped

6 garlic cloves, peeled and roughly chopped

3 Place the wings over the direct heat and cook for 2–3 minutes on each side, until you achieve a nice golden char.

4 Move the wings to the side of the barbecue where there is indirect heat, put the lid over them and cook for 12–15 minutes, until cooked through. To test, insert a skewer into the thickest part of the wing: the juices should run clear.

5 Transfer the cooked wings to a bowl or plate and keep warm.

6 Prepare the hot sauce by blitzing all the ingredients together in a small food processor; any surplus sauce keeps well in the fridge in an airtight container for up to 3 days.

7 Heat the sauce you need in a pan over a medium heat, stirring from time to time for about 10 minutes, until the sauce is reduced a little.

8 Add some of the warmed sauce to the cooked wings, toss to coat and serve sprinkled with sesame seeds and spring onions.

1 Prepare the barbecue by placing a good layer of charcoal evenly across the bottom, then lighting it and waiting until the coals are glowing but have a fine layer of ash on the outside. Pile more of the glowing coals over to one side than the other, to create a heat gradient.

2 While the barbecue is heating, remove the tips from the chicken wings (these can be used for stock), put the remaining wings into a large bowl and season with salt and pepper.

Classic hamburger

DIFFICULTY:

EQUIPMENT: Burger press (optional), barbecue with a lid

SERVES: 4

PREP TIME: 15 minutes, plus 30 minutes chilling

COOKING TIME: 6-8 minutes

The origin of the burger is unclear but may lie with the many migrants who came to the USA during early 20th-century economic boom, and perhaps in particular German settlers from Hamburg. From there it has been dragged up and down the gastronomic spectrum, from mass-produced fast food to its current position as gourmet street-food darling. There are a few hard-and-fast rules when it comes to making your own, although for best results it's worth seeking out meat that has been freshly minced that day. Chuck steak is probably most preferable as it has a great natural layer of fat that will help your burger stay moist and give it that beefy flavour. The unbeatable taste and texture of enriched buns, home-made mustard and ketchup, will also elevate this to restaurant status. Enjoy.

700g/1lb 9oz chuck steak, freshly minced (ground)

salt and ground black pepper

FOR THE SLAW

½ red cabbage, thinly sliced

1 large beetroot (beet), peeled and sliced into matchsticks (wear gloves)

1 red onion, peeled and thinly sliced

1 carrot, peeled and sliced into matchsticks

pinch of sugar

15ml/1 tbsp cider vinegar

30ml/2 tbsp mayonnaise

15ml/1 tbsp Hot Sauce (see page 130)

salt and ground black pepper

TO SERVE

8 rashers of streaky bacon

4 x 25g/1oz slices red Leicester cheese

4 Enriched Buns (see page 58)

Home-made Mustard (see page 131)

Home-made Ketchup (see page 131)

1 Divide the meat into four 175g/6oz portions and shape into round, flat patties, using the bun as a guide – the patties should be slightly larger than the buns to allow for shrinkage. You can use a burger press if you have one.

2 Lightly oil a large plate and put the shaped patties on it. Chill in the fridge for about 30 minutes.

3 Meanwhile, preheat a barbecue with a lid until the coals are white-hot but not flaming.

4 Prepare the slaw by mixing all the ingredients together. Cook the bacon slices on both sides until crisp, then set aside and keep warm.

5 Place the burgers on the hot barbecue and season with a little salt and pepper. Put the lid on and allow the patties to come up to temperature – about 2–3 minutes. Test with a spatula and, when the patties release easily, flip them and continue cooking with the lid down for 2 minutes more. Check for doneness by pushing the centre of the burger: it should be slightly yielding rather than soft.

6 Season the top of the patties with a little salt and pepper, then add a smear of mustard and a slice of cheese. Pop the lid on again to melt the cheese for about 30 seconds.

7 Split the buns and toast them on the barbecue until there's a good char on the split sides

8 Now to build. Place the bases of the buns char side up on plates. Add a little ketchup and mustard, then the patties, bacon and a good spoon of slaw on each. Top with the crowns of the buns and get stuck in. Paper napkins are advisable.

Vegan burger

FOR THE PATTIES

75ml/5 tbsp oil

2 red onions, peeled and finely chopped

5ml/1 tsp each of paprika, ground cumin and ground coriander

100g/3³/₄oz quinoa, cooked according to packet instructions

400g/14oz can of kidney beans, rinsed and drained

400g/14oz can of chickpeas, rinsed and drained

45ml/3 tbsp plain (all-purpose) flour

115g/4oz/1 cup coarse cornmeal

salt and ground black pepper

FOR THE ENRICHED BUNS

375ml/13fl oz/generous 1½ cups almond milk, plus extra for glazing

15g/½oz active dried yeast

5ml/1 tsp sugar

600g/1lb 5oz/5¼ cups strong white bread flour

5ml/1 tsp salt

30ml/2 tbsp coconut oil, melted

mixed sesame seeds and flaky salt, for sprinkling.

FOR THE COLESLAW

45ml/3 tbsp vegan mayonnaise

½ red cabbage, shredded

1 carrot, peeled and grated

1 red onion, peeled and thinly sliced

TO SERVE

Home-made Mustard and Home-made Ketchup (see page 131)

Barbecue Sauce (see page 64)

6 slices of vegan cheese (optional)

1 avocado, stoned, peeled and sliced

There are many great vegan burger options on takeaway menus but this one, made from protein-rich pulses and quinoa and served in a home-made vegan enriched bun, beats them all. If you are craving a bit of authentic barbecue smoke flavour then you can add a touch of liquid smoke to the patty mixture, or simply allow them to char slightly in the pan as you cook them. These vegan buns are really useful for all sorts of dishes, so stash any you don't use in the freezer or double up and make twice the quantity so you can whip up hunger-busting burgers in no time at all.

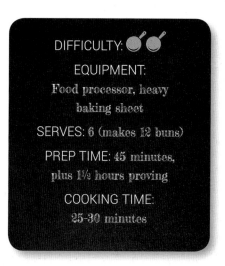

DIFFICULTY:

EQUIPMENT:
Food processor, heavy baking sheet

SERVES: 6 (makes 12 buns)

PREP TIME: 45 minutes, plus 1½ hours proving

COOKING TIME:
25–30 minutes

1 First make the patties. Heat 30ml/ 2 tbsp of the oil in a small pan over a medium heat. Add the onions and a pinch of salt. Allow to cook gently for 6–7 minutes, until the onions are tender and sweet. Tip into a bowl and leave to cool.

2 Put the remaining patty ingredients in a food processor. Add the cooled onions and pulse until it all combines, then taste and adjust the seasoning as necessary. Divide the patties into six balls, put them on a dinner plate and place in the fridge to set.

3 Meanwhile, make the buns. Warm a little of the milk to blood temperature, then add the yeast and sugar and stir to dissolve. Set aside in a warm place for about 10 minutes, until it starts to bubble.

4 Put the flour and salt in a large bowl. Add the yeast mixture, along with remaining milk and the coconut oil. Bring the mixture together until it forms a ball, then tip it out on to a lightly floured surface and knead for 8–10 minutes, until smooth and elastic. Set aside in a lightly oiled bowl, cover with a dish towel and leave to prove in a warm place for about an hour or until doubled in size.

5 When the dough has proved, knock it back (punch it down) with your fist. Tip it out on to a lightly floured surface and knead for 30 seconds. Divide the dough into 12 portions and shape into small balls.

6 Grease a heavy baking sheet and put the balls on it. Loosely cover with clear film (plastic wrap) and leave to prove for 30 minutes, until nearly doubled in size.

7 Brush a little milk over the tops of the buns and sprinkle with seeds and salt. Place a deep roasting tray at the bottom of the oven and preheat the oven to 200ºC/400ºF/Gas 6.

8 Pour a cupful of boiling water into the roasting tray in the oven to create steam. Place the rolls in the oven and bake for about 15 minutes, until golden and risen. Cool on a wire rack.

9 Make the coleslaw by mixing all the ingredients together and seasoning well with salt and pepper.

10 Now cook the patties. Heat the remaining 45ml/3 tbsp of the oil in a large frying pan over a medium heat. Add the shaped patties and cook for 4–5 minutes on each side. Drain on kitchen paper and keep warm.

11 To serve, toast the buns on a dry pan or griddle. Place a dollop of your favourite condiment on the base, then top with slices of cheese if you like, the cooked patties, some coleslaw, maybe some avocado and some more condiments. Serve with more coleslaw on the side.

Hot dog

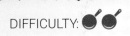

DIFFICULTY: 🍳🍳

EQUIPMENT: Mincer (meat grinder), sausage maker or icing bag, griddle

SERVES: 4-6, with sausages to spare

PREP TIME: 30 minutes, plus chilling

COOKING TIME: 20-25 minutes

The hot dog has to be the ultimate hand-held street food. This recipe reveals how to make your own smoked sausage – a process that is surprisingly easy – for a superlative frankfurter experience. All you need are some sausage casings, top-of-the-range finely minced pork and a piping bag or sausage maker. A cook's cheat is to use liquid smoke in the meat mixture, which gives it an enhanced smoky flavour without having to actually smoke the sausages. Many places claim to serve 'The Best Hot Dogs in the World', including Reykjavik, where Bill Clinton once ordered a hot dog that had everything on it, including raw onions, crispy onions, sweet mustard and a gherkin-flavoured mustard. This recipe has been given the Clinton treatment. I dare anyone to eat two!

FOR THE SAUSAGES

1.2kg/2¹/₂lb pork shoulder, boned and chopped into small cubes

10ml/2 tsp each of garlic powder and finely ground mace

15ml/1 tbsp finely ground black pepper

5ml/1 tsp finely grated nutmeg

30ml/2 tbsp coriander seeds, toasted and ground

5ml/1 tsp allspice berries, finely ground

30ml/2 tbsp salt

15ml/1 tbsp liquid smoke

sausage casings

FOR THE ONIONS

90ml/6 tbsp oil

4 red onions, peeled and thinly sliced

30ml/2 tbsp plain (all-purpose) flour

5ml/1 tsp smoked paprika

salt and ground black pepper

TO SERVE

Enriched Buns (see page 58), formed into hot dog rolls

sauerkraut

3 medium gherkins, finely chopped

Home-made Mustard and Home-made Ketchup (see page 131)

1 To make the sausages, finely mince (grind) all the meat in a mincer and put it into a bowl. Add the spices, seasonings and liquid smoke, really mash everything together well, then set aside.

2 Wash the sausage casings in fresh cold water following the instructions on the packet. Using a piping bag or a sausage maker, stuff the meat mixture into the casings, making twists in the links roughly every 20cm/8in or so.

3 Separate the sausages at the links, cover and refrigerate for at least a couple of hours and up to 5 days. Freeze any sausages you don't need to use right away.

4 When you're ready to eat, drop the sausages into a pan of boiling water and simmer gently for 6–7 minutes, until firm. Drain and pat dry.

5 Prepare the onions. Put 15ml/1 tbsp of the oil in frying pan set over a low-medium heat and add half the onions. Cook for 15 minutes until soft and sticky, stirring occasionally.

6 At the same time, preheat a small frying pan over a medium heat. Mix the flour, paprika, salt and pepper on a large plate and dredge the remaining onions in the flour mixture. Put the remaining oil in the pan and shallow-fry the floured onions for about 10 minutes, until golden and crisp. Drain on kitchen paper.

7 While the onions are cooking, preheat a griddle or frying pan and cook the sausages for 5–6 minutes on each side, until charred.

8 Heat the rolls in a warm oven. Assemble the hot dogs by splitting the rolls lengthways, then adding the sausage, crispy onions, sautéed onions, sauerkraut and chopped gherkins. Top with mustard and ketchup and open wide.

COOK'S TIP
If you're feeding a crowd and up for having a barbecue then these sausages taste even better if they are char-grilled over wood chips rather than in a griddle pan.

Char sui bao with slaw

DIFFICULTY: 🥘🥘

EQUIPMENT: Bamboo steaming basket

MAKES: 18 buns

PREP TIME: 20 minutes, plus 24 hours marinating and 30 minutes resting

COOKING TIME: 2 hours

These Chinese treats – siu bao – consist of salt-cured, soy-braised pork belly served in a soft bun with a crunchy, vinegary pickle and are a really popular grab-and-go snack that street-food aficionados the world over have fallen in love with – with the result that the buns are becoming more widely available in supermarkets as well as in speciality Asian supermarkets and online. This recipe makes enough for 18 people so it's ideal for a party or large gathering since the prep can be done in advance and as your guests arrive they are quick to warm through and assemble. However, if you don't need that many in one go then the buns freeze remarkably well and are pretty quick to thaw.

1.56kg/3½lb pork belly, skin removed (ask your butcher to do this)

15ml/1 tbsp flaky sea salt

45ml/3 tbsp light soy sauce

50g/2oz/4 tbsp dark muscovado sugar

2 whole star anise

FOR THE PICKLE

4 small Lebanese cucumbers, sliced

2 carrots, peeled and sliced into matchsticks

45ml/3 tbsp white wine vinegar

15ml/1 tbsp caster (superfine) sugar

5ml/1 tsp salt

TO SERVE

6 spring onions (scallions), finely sliced

3 fresh red chillies, finely sliced (optional)

sriracha or other chilli sauce

1 Put the pork on a large roasting tray or pan (whatever it fits into), sprinkle with salt and leave in the fridge for about a day.

2 When you are ready to cook, preheat the oven to 220ºC/425ºF/Gas 7.

3 Mix the soy sauce, sugar and star anise together and rub all over the pork. Put the pork in the roasting tray or pan belly side up and cook it in the hot oven for 20 minutes. Lower the temperature to 110ºC/225ºF/Gas 1/4, cover the roasting tray tightly with foil, and continue cooking for about another 1½ hours.

4 Set aside in a warm spot to relax for about 30 minutes, still covered with foil. When ready to serve, slice the pork into 5mm/¼in-thick slices.

5 Shortly before serving, make the pickle by mixing all the ingredients together in a small bowl.

6 Warm the buns in a bamboo steamer for 2–3 minutes. Open the buns and fill with some pickle and sliced pork, then top with sliced spring onions, fresh chilli, if using, and sriracha or chilli sauce.

COOK'S TIPS

• If you find yourself with some leftover meat it can stored in the fridge for up to 5 days. To reheat, wrap it in foil and warm it through at 140ºC/275ºf/Gas 1 for about 30 minutes.
• Try to seek out good-quality outdoor-reared pork that has a good coating of fat and slightly firm and dry flesh.
• Make sure you use light soy sauce. A rule of thumb is light soy sauce for cooking and dark soy sauce for dipping.

Texas-style barbecue beef

3kg/6lb 9oz slow-aged whole piece of brisket (see Cook's Tips)

Enriched Buns (see page 58), to serve

FOR THE RUB

5ml/1 tsp each of coriander seeds, black peppercorns and cumin seeds

10ml/2 tsp each of fennel seeds and paprika

10ml/2 tsp salt

45ml/3 tbsp dark muscovado sugar

FOR THE BARBECUE SAUCE

30ml/2 tbsp oil

2 red onions, peeled and finely chopped

3 garlic cloves, peeled and crushed

5ml/1 tsp English mustard powder

10ml/2 tsp paprika

5ml/1 tsp ground ginger

30ml/2 tbsp tomato paste

10ml/2 tsp yeast extract

60ml/4 tbsp bourbon

45ml/3 tbsp tamarind paste (made according to the packet instructions)

400ml/14fl oz/1²⁄₃ cups passata (bottled strained tomatoes)

30ml/2 tbsp pomegranate molasses

45ml/3 tbsp cider vinegar

30ml/2 tbsp apricot jam

45ml/3 tbsp dark muscovado sugar

2 bay leaves

FOR THE COLESLAW

45ml/3 tbsp cider vinegar

pinch of sugar

30ml/2 tbsp finely grated fresh root ginger

1 large beetroot (beet), peeled and sliced into matchsticks (wear gloves)

2 carrots, peeled and sliced into matchsticks

½ red cabbage, finely shredded

3 spring onions (scallions), finely sliced

salt and ground black pepper

Brisket comes from the lower chest of the cow. It is full of wonderful connective tissue that, when cooked slowly, renders into soft, delicious, flavoursome meat that cries out to be sandwiched in a soft bun and slathered with a complex hot, sweet and sour sauce. A simple domestic kettle barbecue will give you the desired effect but a kamado (charcoal-fired grill) will allow you to cook at a consistently low, controllable temperature without having to stoke the fire. Use good-quality lump-wood charcoal placed indirectly over the coals in order to give the meat a slightly smoky barbecue flavour. See Cook's Tips for how to cook this in the oven.

DIFFICULTY:

EQUIPMENT: Barbecue or kamado with a lid, mortar and pestle or mini food processor

SERVES: 10-12

PREP TIME: 20-30 minutes, plus time to heat the barbecue

COOKING TIME: 7-8 hours

1 Remove the meat from the fridge about an hour before cooking. Pat dry with kitchen paper. Preheat a barbecue with a tight-fitting lid, or a kamado smoker. Allow the temperature to come up to about 100°C/212°F.

2 Blitz together all the ingredients for the rub in a mini food processor or bash together with a mortar and pestle. This can be done in advance and kept in an airtight jar or container.

3 Using your hands, press the rub mixture on to the surface of the meat.

4 Place the meat on the grill (broiler) rack, ensuring that the meat is not in contact with the flames. Close the lid and cook for 7–8 hours, keeping an eye on the temperature, stoking the fire when necessary and flipping the meat round from time to time.

5 When cooked, the meat should be yielding to the touch and cave effortlessly. At this stage, remove it from the heat and keep it wrapped in foil (to hold the juices in) until you're ready to serve.

6 While the meat is cooking, make the sauce by heating the oil in a

heavy pan. Add the onions and cook for about 10 minutes, until softened. Add the garlic and cook for a further 2 minutes. Stir in all the remaining ingredients. Simmer over a medium heat for 25–30 minutes, until reduced, then season to taste.

7 Remove the bay leaf, then blend the sauce and pass it through a sieve into a clean jug. Pour the sauce into a warmed sterilised bottle (see page 16) or container and seal – you should have more than enough.

8 To make the coleslaw, combine the vinegar, sugar and ginger in a large bowl, then add all the vegetables and seasoning and stir to combine well. This can sit for a while to allow the flavours to develop.

9 Toast the buns lightly on a griddle or in a dry frying pan. Slice the brisket into generous 2cm/1/2in slices, lay on the base of the buns and top with coleslaw and barbecue sauce. Finish with the crown of the bun and give it a good squish to hold it all

COOK'S TIPS

• Look for a good layer of yellowish fat on the surface of the brisket. This will help to baste the meat as the fat renders, thus flavouring it during the cooking process. Ask your butcher for the 'point' or 'button' end of the brisket, which is slightly thicker.

• To cook the brisket in the oven, preheat it to 220ºC/425ºF/Gas 7, add the meat and immediately turn the temperature down to 100ºC/212ºF/Gas 1/4. Cook in the same way as you would on a barbecue or kamado

Hot salt beef on rye

DIFFICULTY: 🍳🍳

EQUIPMENT: Large, heavy frying pan or skillet

SERVES: 2

PREP TIME: 5 minutes plus 1 hour soaking

COOKING TIME: 1¼–1¾ hours.

In New York this sandwich is known as the Reuben and is thought to have been introduced to the USA by the migrant Jewish community. It is the most delicious concoction, combining the cornerstones of our taste buds, with sweet pickle, salty beef, sour sauerkraut, bitter caraway seeds and umami cheese. The beef is a joint of brisket, which has been brined (soaked in salted water) for up to two weeks, after this process it is sometimes called corned beef, particularly in Ireland and the USA, but shouldn't be confused with the stuff that comes in tins. It is possible to order salted beef from butchers or some supermarkets, in which case all you have to do is gently poach the joint in water. Look out for a rye bread that contains a mix of rye flour and strong wheat flour with caraway. Traditionally, rye has little gluten so the wheat flour will add airiness to the bread, making your sandwich lighter and crispy.

1kg/2¼lb salt beef brisket joint (see Cook's Tip)

4 slices rye bread

softened salted butter, for spreading

4 slices Emmenthal cheese

115g/4oz/1 cup cooked sauerkraut

Home-made Mustard (see page 131) and sliced gherkins, to serve

1 Soak the salted beef in plenty of cold water for about 1 hour. Rinse really well and place it in a pan with cold water to cover. Add spices if you wish (see Cook's Tip). Slowly bring to the boil and simmer gently with a lid on for about 1–1½ hours. To check for doneness, insert a roasting fork into the centre of the beef. If it is cooked it should easily slide out. You can cook this way ahead of time and then simply reheat the beef in the cooking liquid. (And on that note, the cooking liquid makes a delicious soup or sauce, so don't tip it away.)

2 Lift out the meat and slice it generously. Lay the slices of bread on a large chopping board and butter each on one side.

3 Lay a slice of cheese on the unbuttered side of each slice of bread. Top with thick slices of meat and a couple of spoonfuls of sauerkraut. Dollop a couple of generous tablespoons of mustard on the other unbuttered sides of the bread, along with a little more sauerkraut.

4 Sandwich the slices together with the buttered sides on the outside.

5 Preheat a large, heavy frying pan or skillet over a medium heat. Place the sandwiches in the pan, compress with a heavy pan on top and cook for about 4–5 minutes per side, until golden and crunchy and the cheese is starting to melt.

6 Drain a little on kitchen paper and serve with mustard and gherkins.

COOK'S TIP

Ask your butcher whether the salt beef has been brined with or without spices and flavourings. If without, then you could add the following to the poaching water: 1 peeled onion, 3 bay leaves, 2 tsp each of coriander seeds, dill seeds, black peppercorns and mustard seeds, 1 tsp allspice berries, 6 cloves and 1 star anise.

Grilled cheese sandwich

Sold at street-food trucks, festivals and winter food markets in many parts of the world, this hand-held sandwich is very much open to experimentation in terms of the types of cheese, hams/charcuterie and bread used, and could even feature an egg on top (à la croque-madam). Typically, a croque-monsieur will have the cheese on the outside but the method given here seals and envelopes the filling with a crisp exterior instead, making it easier to handle. This recipe uses goat's cheese and beetroot – tried-and-tested flavour friends – and the walnuts and honey bring an extra level of sweet and sour. For a touch of decadence, drizzle with truffle oil, or add some chopped cornichon to cut through the rich cheese.

DIFFICULTY:

SPECIAL EQUIPMENT:
Large, heavy frying pan or skillet

SERVES: 2

PREP TIME: 5 minutes

COOKING TIME: 10 minutes

salted butter, softened
4 slices good-quality sourdough bread
150g/5oz/10tbsp soft goat's cheese
200g/7oz cooked beetroot, sliced
115g/4oz/1 cup shelled walnuts, chopped
45ml/3 tbsp local honey

COOK'S TIP
You can fiddle around with various beetroot flavour varieties that are now being produced, such as my current favourite – chilli and balsamic vinegar.

1 Preheat a large 30cm/12in (approx) frying pan over a low-medium heat.

2 On a board, butter the bread on one side and lay all four slices buttered side down.

3 Spread about half of the cheese on to two of the slices of bread, then add a little of the sliced beetroot, some walnuts and a drizzle of honey.

4 Top with the other slices of bread, leaving the buttered side facing up. Press firmly, and carefully slide into the hot pan.

5 Cook for about 5 minutes per side, until the outside is crisp and golden and the cheese is melted. To give some extra contact and ensure even browning, press down lightly with a spatula.

6 Remove the sandwich from the pan and drain on kitchen paper. Slice in half and serve straight away.

Lahmacun

DIFFICULTY: 🍳🍳

EQUIPMENT: Pizza stone (optional) or a large, heavy baking sheet

SERVES: 6

PREP TIME: 30 minutes, plus 1 hour proving

COOKING TIME: 35-45 minutes

This tasty little Anatolian treat – a close relative of the Italian's pizza – is usually served as a hot meze dish in Turkey, but it makes a fantastic snack or lunch in its own right. Essentially a flatbread topped with a really well seasoned meaty, tomatoey, lemony paste, it is finished with a squirt of lemon juice and a strewing of nubbly toasted pine nuts and chopped parsley for a gastronomic flourish that really gets the taste buds going. You can use a pizza oven to make this but a conventional oven will also do the job – just get it really hot. A pizza stone will help matters.

FOR THE FLATBREADS

10g/¼oz active dried yeast

pinch of sugar

175ml/6fl oz/¾ cup warm water

450g/1lb/4 cups strong white bread flour

pinch of salt

15ml/1 tbsp olive oil, plus extra for greasing

FOR THE TOPPING

15ml/1 tbsp olive oil

1 red onion, peeled and finely chopped

2 garlic cloves, peeled and crushed

pinch of cinnamon

5ml/1 tsp ground cumin

225g/8oz lean minced (ground) lamb

45ml/3 tbsp tomato paste

pinch of dried red chilli flakes

5ml/1 tsp dried mint

15ml/1 tbsp sumac

salt and ground black pepper

TO SERVE

lemon wedges

handful of chopped fresh flat leaf parsley

handful of pine nuts, lightly toasted

1 Make the flatbread dough by mixing the yeast and sugar together in a small bowl with a little of the warm water. Set aside and leave for about 10 minutes, until frothy.

2 Mix the flour, salt and oil together in a large bowl. Make a well or dip in the middle, slowly add the yeast mixture and then the remaining water and draw the flour in with your hands. Mix to a smooth dough.

3 Tip the dough on to a lightly floured clean surface and knead for 5–10 minutes, until smooth, soft and elastic. You could also use a dough hook on a food processor – knead for about 5 minutes.

4 Lightly grease the bowl with a little oil, add the dough, cover with clear film (plastic wrap) and put in a warm place for about an hour, until the dough has doubled in size.

5 Meanwhile, make the topping. Put the oil in a heavy pan over a medium heat, then add the onions and cook for about 10 minutes, until soft and translucent. Add the garlic and cook for a further minute before stirring in the spices.

6 Add the lamb and cook for 4–5 minutes, until coloured. Mix in the tomato paste, chilli flakes, mint, sumac and plenty of salt and pepper and stir fry for another 1 minute. Remove from the heat.

7 Once the dough is proved, put the pizza stone or a large, heavy baking sheet in the oven and preheat it to 220ºC/425ºF/Gas 7.

8 Take the dough and knock it back (punch it down) with your fist. Divide the mixture into six balls. On a lightly floured surface roll out the balls to ovals that are roughly 15cm/6in long by 7.5cm/3in wide.

9 Divide the minced lamb mixture into six and spread a portion on each oval. Lift a couple of ovals on to the pizza stone or baking sheet and bake for 8–10 minutes, until golden and crisp. Remove from the oven and keep warm while you cook the remaining breads.

10 Finish with a squeeze of lemon, a flourish of chopped parsley and a casual scatter of toasted pine nuts, to complete the effortless look! Serve warm.

5ml/1 tsp each of black peppercorns, fennel seeds, cumin seeds and fenugreek seeds

15ml/1 tbsp coriander seeds

2.5ml/½ tsp each of ground cinnamon, ground cardamom and ground cloves

pinch of ground nutmeg

2 tsp salt

15ml/1 tbsp each of paprika and sumac

400g/14oz/scant 2 cups natural (plain) yogurt

2–2½ kg/4½–5lb leg of lamb (about 1.2kg/2½lb without the bone)

FOR THE TAHINI SAUCE

100ml/7 tbsp tahini

3 garlic cloves, peeled and crushed

200g/7oz/scant 1 cup natural (plain) yogurt

lemon juice, to taste

salt and ground black pepper

For the onion salad:

2 red onions, peeled and sliced

handful of fresh parsley leaves, chopped

7.5ml/½ tbsp sumac

TO SERVE

Arabic flat breads

45ml/3 tbsp harissa paste

2 Lebanese cucumbers, sliced

3 tomatoes, diced

pickled chillies

cold beers (optional)

VARIATION

Shwarmas also work well with boneless chicken thighs stacked on a skewer and marinated in the same sauce. They take far less time to cook of course, so stand over them. And don't worry about burnt ends either, they're the best bits.

The origin of the schwarma seems to be rooted in eastern Turkey, where stacks of seasoned meat are layered on top of each other and cooked vertically on a rotating grill. Although the actual style of cooking is tricky to replicate at home, this recipe for succulent marinated and barbecued whole leg of lamb comes very close to the original in terms of flavour, and the meat is likely to be of a much higher standard. Lamb is perfect here because its high fat content means it will render and self-baste as it cooks. The bread I have used here is an Arabic flat bread that you should be able to find in supermarkets or specialist Middle Eastern stores.

DIFFICULTY: 🍳🍳

EQUIPMENT: Mortar and pestle or mini food processor, tray or tub with a lid, barbecue

SERVES: 4-6

PREP TIME: 25-30 minutes, plus overnight marinating and 30 minutes resting

COOKING TIME: 4 hours

1 Toast the peppercorns and all the whole seeds together in a dry frying pan over a medium heat for 1–2 minutes, until you can smell the aromas. Remove from the pan and crush with a mortar and pestle or blitz in a mini food processor.

2 Mix all the spices together with the salt and the yogurt. Rub the spice mix into the lamb. Place on a tray or in a tub with a lid, cover and refrigerate overnight.

3 The next day, remove the lamb from the fridge about 1 hour before cooking. Preheat a barbecue so the coals are glowing embers.

4 Place the lamb on to the barbecue with the fat side facing upwards and cook for about 30 minutes. Wrap the lamb in foil and cook for about another 3½ hours. Top up the charcoal as necessary, but remember that we want to do this low and slow.

5 When the lamb is done, allow it to rest for 30 minutes still wrapped in the foil before carving.

6 While the meat is resting, make the tahini sauce by mixing everything together – it should have a sharp, garlicky lemon fizz to it so adjust the lemon level as required.

7 Make the onion salad by mixing everything together in a little bowl.

8 To serve, brush the inside of the breads with a little harissa paste and warm them on the grill. Fill with sliced lamb, onion salad, cucumbers, tomatoes and pickled chillies, then drizzle with a little tahini sauce, roll and enjoy with cold beers.

Pork burritos

2kg/4½lb boneless pork shoulder, skin removed (ask your butcher to do this)

10ml/2 tsp each of dried oregano and smoked paprika

60ml/4 tbsp chipotle paste

salt and ground black pepper

FOR THE BLACK BEANS

30ml/2 tbsp oil

3 garlic cloves, peeled and crushed

5ml/1 tsp ground cumin

100ml/3½fl oz/scant ½ cup chicken stock

400g/14oz canned kidney beans, drained and rinsed

salt and ground black pepper

FOR THE ACCOMPANIMENTS

15ml/1 tbsp oil

2 red onions, peeled and thinly sliced

2 sweet red (bell) peppers, seeded and sliced into thin strips

4 (or as many as you dare) fresh jalapeño chillies, sliced

about 4 limes

2.5ml/½ tsp smoked paprika

2 ripe avocados, stoned and peeled

pinch of ancho chilli flakes

2 tomatoes, finely chopped

½ red onion, peeled and finely chopped

handful of chopped fresh coriander (cilantro)

salt and ground black pepper

TO SERVE

soft tortillas

sour cream

60ml/4 tbsp fresh coriander (cilantro) leaves, chopped

60ml/4 tbsp grated mature (sharp) Cheddar cheese

A simple dish to assemble once all the component parts are ready, the only special equipment you may need is a large armchair in which to sit down and digest your food – the slow-cooked pork and comforting black beans encased in a soft tortilla shell can ease you into a food-induced stupor. That said, the freshness and fieriness of the various toppings really help to cut through the rich meat and bring some welcome texture to the offering.

You can make your own tortillas for a really authentic touch or simply buy them fresh – flour, blue corn or plain corn, it's entirely up to you. I have opted for soft wheat-flour tortillas. The pulled pork part is a relatively simple affair that involves slow-cooking pork shoulder in chipotle paste until the meat is melting and falls apart with the touch of a spoon!

DIFFICULTY:

EQUIPMENT: N/A

SERVES: 8-10

PREP TIME: 30 minutes, plus 30 minutes resting

COOKING TIME: 4-5 hours

1 Preheat the oven to 110ºC/225ºF/ Gas ¼. Rub the pork shoulder all over with oregano, paprika, chipotle paste and a little salt. Place in a small roasting tray and cook slowly for about 4–5 hours, until the meat has a lot of give in it.

2 Cover with foil and leave to rest for about 30 minutes before pulling with a couple of forks to shred. Keep the meat warm.

3 To make the black beans, heat the oil in a small pan over a medium heat. Add the garlic and cumin and move around in the pan for 1–2 minutes. Add the chicken stock and the beans. Cover and cook for 10–15 minutes, until the beans are starting to give. Season with salt and pepper.

4 Meanwhile, prepare the accompaniments. Heat the oil in a frying pan over a medium heat. Add the sliced red onions, the peppers and all but 1 of the jalapeños, cook for a minute or two until the mix has slightly tinged and wilted, then add the juice of half a lime, smoked paprika and

seasoning. Set aside and keep warm until ready to use.

5 Crush the avocados with a fork, season with a little lime juice, chilli flakes and salt and pepper. Set aside.

6 Mix the chopped tomatoes with the remaining chopped red onion and a little lime juice. Add the remaining jalapeño pepper and some chopped coriander and mix well.

7 Once all the fillings and accompaniments are ready, heat the tortillas for about 20 seconds in a dry pan. I like a little char on them but to achieve it you have to work quickly as they go hard and split when rolled if left for too long.

8 Lay out a tortilla, then add a spoonful of black beans, a good spoonful of pulled pork, and some of the onion and peppers. Top with a little avocado, tomato and onion salad, sour cream, and a sprinkle each of fresh coriander and grated cheese.

9 Fold part of the tortilla over the filling, then roll the tortilla away from you until you reach the end, sealing in the filling. You can wrap it in foil or greaseproof paper if you are on the go, but I'd suggest you eat it swiftly and use a napkin.

VARIATIONS
- This also works with beef short ribs, boned lamb shoulder and chicken thighs. Cooking times will vary.
- If I've got a barbecue on the go then I'll usually give the pork a whirl over the coals either at the beginning or at the end of the cooking process, for a hit of smokiness.

Sis kebab

1 kg/2¼lb leg or loin of lamb, fat removed and cubed (ask your butcher to do this)

3 tbsp/45ml olive oil

juice of 2 lemons

5ml/1 tsp each of fresh thyme leaves and dried oregano

pickled chillies

3 red onions, peeled and cut into quarters

3 green (bell) peppers, seeded and cut into large cubes

6 bay leaves

salt and ground black pepper

6 flat breads, to serve

½ red cabbage, finely shredded, to serve

FOR THE GARLIC SAUCE

2 heads of garlic, peeled and chopped

small bunch of parsley, chopped

1 egg white

200ml/7fl oz/scant 1 cup olive oil

juice of 2 lemons

salt and ground black pepper

FOR THE HOT SAUCE

olive oil

3 garlic cloves, peeled and crushed

1 red onion, peeled and roughly chopped

1 red pepper, seeded and roughly chopped

3 fresh green chillies, seeded and roughly chopped

400g/14oz canned plum tomatoes

pinch of sugar

salt and ground black pepper

FOR THE ONION SALAD

2 red onions, peeled and thinly sliced

handful of chopped fresh parsley leaves

15ml/1 tbsp sumac

Proper sis kebabs are a world away from the greasy takeaway offerings often consumed late at night to soak up an excess of alcohol. Home-made ones consist of juicy, carefully spiced cubed or minced meat that is threaded on to long metal skewers and cooked over hot coals before being folded inside soft bread with cool garlic sauce, astringent pickled veg and a liberal shake of hot sauce. Easy to make, they are great for feeding a crowd at a barbecue since all the prep is done in advance and guests can just help themselves and compile their own favourite combinations.

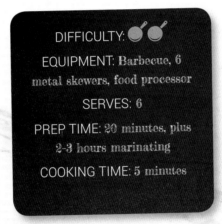

DIFFICULTY: 🍳🍳

EQUIPMENT: Barbecue, 6 metal skewers, food processor

SERVES: 6

PREP TIME: 20 minutes, plus 2-3 hours marinating

COOKING TIME: 5 minutes

1 Put the lamb in a large bowl and add the oil, lemon juice, thyme, oregano and salt and pepper. Slice the squeezed lemons into quarters to use as bookends on the skewers. Cover the meat and leave it to sit for 2–3 hours.

2 About 30 minutes before the end of the marinating time, prepare a charcoal grill or barbecue.

3 Thread a pickled chilli onto each skewer, then add the lamb, interspersing chunks of meat with onion or pepper pieces. Finish with a lemon wedge and a bay leaf.

4 Prepare the garlic sauce by putting all the ingredients apart from the oil and lemon juice into a food processor. Blend until smooth.

5 Slowly trickle the olive oil into the food processor in a thin, steady stream until the sauce thickens. Check the seasoning and add lemon juice to taste. Transfer to a serving bowl and give the food processor a quick rinse.

6 To make the hot sauce, blend all the ingredients together in the food processor, seasoning well. Transfer to a serving bowl. For the onion salad, combine everything in a small bowl.

7 To cook the meat, place the skewers over the hot coals and cook, turning frequently, for 4–5 minutes, until ridged with char marks. Remove and keep warm.

8 Warm the flat breads and then fill with plenty of crunchy cabbage, add a little of the meat, some of the onion salad, a pickled chilli and a dollop of each of the sauces to your taste.

Cornish pasties

DIFFICULTY: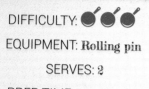

EQUIPMENT: Rolling pin

SERVES: 2

PREP TIME: 30 minutes, plus about 30 minutes chilling

COOKING TIME: 45-50 minutes

FOR THE PASTRY

175g/6oz/1½ cups strong white bread flour

pinch of salt

60ml/4 tbsp cold butter, cut into small cubes

30ml/2 tbsp cold lard (white cooking fat), cut into small cubes

30-45ml/2-3 tbsp cold water

FOR THE FILLING

1 large onion, peeled

1 large waxy potato, peeled

¼ small swede, peeled

250g/9oz skirt beef steak

few drops of Worcestershire sauce

15ml/1 tbsp water

large pinch of thyme leaves

pinch each of salt, mustard powder and ground black pepper

2 generous knobs of butter

1 egg, beaten

Home-made Mustard (see page 131), to serve

The origin story of these iconic hand-held snacks is well known, and since those infamous tin-mining times their popularity and availability has grown phenomenally. And little wonder: crisp golden pastry encasing a piping-hot filling of well-seasoned meat and veg is a treat that few can resist – from cyclists in the saddle to football fans in the stands, they are the ultimate portable meal. There is a world of difference, however, between limp, lardy commercially produced pasties and the real deal and, other than heading down to Cornwall, the only way to guarantee the ultimate pasty experience is to make your own.

1 To make the pastry, sift the flour into a large bowl. Stir in the salt, then add the butter and lard and use your fingertips to work the fat into the flour until you have something that resembles fine breadcrumbs. Add a couple of tablespoons of cold water to form a moist but not too sticky ball of dough. Press the dough into a flat circle, wrap in clear film (plastic wrap) and chill it in the fridge for 30 minutes.

2 Meanwhile, chop the potatoes as uniformly as you can into 1cm/1/2in cubes. Chop the swede in the same way. Slice the beef into slivers; we want everything to cook at the same time, so cutting the meat finely is really important.

3 Mix all the veggies and meat well, then add the Worcestershire sauce, water, thyme and a good pinch each of salt, mustard and plenty of black pepper – you want to taste the pepper!

4 Take the pastry from the fridge, divide it into two and put it on a lightly floured surface. Roll out to two circles, each measuring about 20-23cm/8-9in in diameter.

5 Place half the filling mixture on the centre of one circle, leaving a rim of pastry measuring about 2.5cm/1in. Put a generous knob of butter in the middle. Repeat with the other pasty.

6 Brush beaten egg all round the rims of the pasties. Fold the pastry over to form half-moon shapes and encase the filling, then seal the edges by pressing down and crimping the edges between your fingers. The Cornish say between 16–20 is about the right number of crimps, but if you'd rather just go round the edge of the pastry with the tines of a fork then that's fine.

7 Cut a little vent in the top of each pasty to allow steam to escape, then put them on a heavy baking sheet lined with baking parchment. Brush well with beaten egg and allow to dry in the fridge while you heat the oven. For a pro finish, you can do this twice.

8 Preheat the oven to 160ºC/325ºF/ Gas 3. Place the baking sheet in the centre of the oven and bake the pasties for 45–50 minutes, until golden and slightly risen. Allow the pasties to cool a little before serving with home-made mustard.

Scotch eggs

DIFFICULTY: 🍳🍳

EQUIPMENT: Deep-fryer or large, heavy pan suitable for deep-frying

SERVES: 4

PREP TIME: 30 minutes, plus 10-15 minutes chilling

COOKING TIME: 25 minutes

Thought to have been created at Fortnum & Mason in London, the ultimate Scotch egg will be crispy on the outside, contain a toothsome meaty layer and have a slightly soft egg yolk in the middle. I like to go one stage further and have a warm and runny egg yolk, but you might prefer it firm. I like to use duck eggs as they are super-rich and a little less temperature sensitive than hen's eggs. It is a bit time consuming, and fiddly, to make your own Scotch eggs, but you can make them in advance and cook just before serving. Panko breadcrumbs give the golden outer coating extra crunch. Serve with home-made mustard or some piccalilli to cut through the richness.

4 duck eggs

500g/1¼lb pork sausage meat

5ml/1 tsp fresh thyme leaves

15ml/1 tbsp chopped fresh sage leaves

pinch each of ground nutmeg and ground mace

large pinch of English mustard powder

3 eggs, beaten

115g/4oz/1 cup plain (all-purpose) flour

115g/4oz/2 cups panko breadcrumbs

salt and ground black pepper

oil, for deep-frying

Home-made Mustard (see page 131) and chopped chives, to serve

1 To cook the eggs, bring a large pan of water to a rolling boil. Lower the eggs gently into the water, reduce the heat to a simmer and cook for 5 minutes.

2 Meanwhile, prepare a bowl of iced cold water. As soon as the eggs are ready, scoop them into it using a slotted spoon. Leave the eggs to cool until warm, topping up the ice cubes if they melt quickly. Peel the eggs, then leave them in the cold water until you're ready to use them.

3 Meanwhile, prepare the meat layer by putting the sausage meat in a bowl. Add the herbs, spices, mustard powder and a good pinch of salt and pepper. Mix well and divide into four even balls. Use weighing scales to check, as you want the finished Scotch eggs to be the same size so they cook in the same amount of time.

4 Flatten the balls into fairly flat discs using the palm of your hand. Place the boiled eggs on the centre of the flattened patty. Use the sausage meat to surround the egg, making sure it is completely coated in meat. Pinch any open areas to seal.

5 Put the egg, flour and breadcrumbs on to separate plates and have an empty one ready for the coated Scotch eggs. Dredge the sausage ball through the flour, shake off any excess and then roll it in the egg, ensuring it is well coated. Lastly, roll it in the breadcrumbs until it is completely coated. Place the finished eggs on the empty plate. I usually double dip the eggs, so repeat the process, if you like.

6 Put the finished eggs in the fridge for about 10–15 minutes to set.

7 Meanwhile, preheat the oven to 150ºC/300ºF/Gas 2. Pour the oil in a deep-fryer or large, heavy pan suitable for deep-frying and heat it to 190ºC/375ºF. Working with two at a time, lower the eggs into the hot oil and cook for about 5 minutes, until golden. Transfer to a baking sheet and repeat the deep-frying with the other eggs. Bake all the eggs in the hot oven for 8 minutes.

8 Remove from the oven, slice in half while still warm and serve immediately with a dollop of mustard and sprinkled with chives.

Ultimate nachos

FOR THE PICO DE GALLO

250g/9oz mixed tomatoes, finely chopped

1 fresh jalapeño, finely chopped

1 small red onion, peeled and finely chopped

good squeeze of lime juice

handful of fresh coriander (cilantro), chopped

salt and ground black pepper

FOR THE AVOCADO CREAM

2 avocados

juice of 1 lime

2.5ml/½ tsp ancho chilli flakes

75ml/5 tbsp sour cream

salt and ground black pepper

FOR THE TORTILLA CHIPS

8 fresh corn tortillas

oil, for deep-frying

chilli powder and lime zest, for sprinkling

FOR THE CHEESE SAUCE

115g/4oz/1 cup grated Cheddar cheese

pinch of ground turmeric

90ml/6 tbsp double (heavy) cream

90ml/6 tbsp milk

5ml/1 tsp cornflour (cornstarch)

handful of fresh chives, chopped

salt and ground black pepper

TO SERVE

fresh chives and fresh coriander (cilantro), chopped

spring onions (scallions), chopped

pickled chillies

Nothing beats nachos for a night in watching a movie – the combination of runny cheese, hot (in both senses) tortilla chips, sharp and zingy tomato and onion salad (pico de gallo) and smooth avocado sauce is so satisfying and beats boring old potato crisps any day. Set this up on a little tray with all the dipping accompaniments in bowls, then just before you want to start the movie bring out the tortilla chips and cheese sauce from the oven, so they are piping hot. You can make the chips extra large if you wish for extra scooping potential.

DIFFICULTY:

EQUIPMENT: Food processor, deep-fryer or a large, heavy pan suitable for deep-frying

SERVES: 2

PREP TIME: 20 minutes

COOKING TIME: 10–15 minutes

1 Combine all the ingredients for the pico de gallo in a small serving bowl. Test for lime, chilli and seasoning and adjust to suit your taste.

2 Place all the ingredients for the avocado cream in a food processor and blend until smooth. Taste and adjust the seasoning, then scrape into a dipping bowl.

3 To make the chips, lay the tortillas out in a stack on a chopping board and slice them into wedges. Heat the oven to 110°C/225°F/Gas ¼. Heat the oil to 160°C/325°F in a deep-fryer or large, heavy pan suitable for deep-frying. Test whether it is ready by putting a piece of bread in the oil. If it spits and fizzes, the oil is ready.

4 Fry the chips in batches in the hot oil for 2–3 minutes, turning them gently. Remove and drain on kitchen paper, then sprinkle with a little chilli powder and lime zest. Set aside in an ovenproof serving dish in the oven to keep warm.

5 Make the cheese sauce by putting all the ingredients in a small pan set over a medium heat. Allow the cheese to gently melt and stir until it all comes together. Check the seasoning (you may not need any extra salt).

6 Just before you are ready to eat, pour the cheese sauce over the tortilla chips. Serve on a tray with the rest of the dips, sprinkled with the herbs and spring onions, and with pickled chillies on the side.

Fish & triple-cooked chips

1.6kg/3½lb potatoes (see Cook's Tip)

4 x 175g/6oz white fish fillets (we used haddock), skin on

oil, for deep-frying

FOR THE BATTER

400g/14oz/3½ cups plain (all-purpose) flour

300ml/½ pint/1¼ cups dark ale (try to find one that is fresh and lively)

15g/½oz easy-blend (rapid-rise) yeast

5ml/1 tsp honey

5ml/1 tsp curry powder

salt and ground black pepper

FOR THE TARTARE SAUCE

115g/4oz/½ cup good-quality mayonnaise

15ml/1 tbsp each of chopped capers, gherkins and fresh parsley

FOR THE MUSHY PEAS

15ml/1 tbsp oil

1 onion, peeled and finely chopped

2 garlic cloves, peeled and crushed

150ml/¼ pint/⅔ cup double (heavy) cream

225g/8oz/2 cups frozen peas, thawed

5ml/1 tsp chopped fresh mint (optional)

salt and ground black pepper

TO SERVE

bread and butter, sea salt, malt vinegar, lemon wedges

COOK'S TIP

I like waxy potatoes such as Charlotte, Apache or Cypriot as I find they hold together better, but you could choose a floury sort like Maris Piper if you prefer.

A national dish in the UK, 'fish and chips' means different things to different people. Regional variations include the type of fish, whether it is fried in meat dripping or vegetable oil, and what it's served with: ketchup, curry sauce, gravy, pickled eggs, bread and butter, cup of tea, mushy peas, malt vinegar, tartar sauce, a glass of white wine... Triple-cooked chips make for a truly decadent eating experience. They require some time and patience, but you can stop at the end of step 5, portion up the par-cooked chips and stockpile them in the freezer for fast-food convenience in your own home.

DIFFICULTY: ● ● ●

EQUIPMENT: Deep-fryer or a large, heavy pan suitable for deep-frying, stick blender

SERVES: 4

PREP TIME: 20 minutes, plus 5 hours chilling and freezing (for the chips)

COOKING TIME: 50–60 minutes

1 Peel the potatoes, or leave the skins on if you prefer. Chop into thick batons about 2cm/¾in wide.

2 Put the potatoes in a steamer set over a pan of simmering water and steam them for 10–15 minutes, until just tender. Set aside until just cool enough to handle.

3 Line two baking sheets with baking paper, making sure the trays fit in your fridge and freezer. Place the potatoes on the baking sheets, leaving a little space between each one. Chill for 2 hours or until firm.

4 When you're ready to cook, heat the oil to 130°C/266°F in a deep-fryer or large, heavy pan suitable for deep-frying. In small batches, gently lower the chips into the hot oil and cook for 4 minutes.

5 Drain and gently place on the lined baking sheets. Repeat until all the chips have been blanched in the oil. If you wish, at this stage you can place the trays in the freezer and freeze for about 3 hours until firm. The chips can then be portioned, bagged up and kept in the freezer on stand-by.

6 Now prepare the fish batter. Put 300g/10oz/2½ cups of the flour and a pinch of salt in a large mixing bowl. Make a well in the middle and pour in the beer. Pour the yeast into the mixture, add the honey and curry powder and bring the mixture together with a whisk. It should be smooth, with the consistency of thick cream. If it is lumpy, buzz it with a stick blender. Leave it to rest for about 20 minutes.

7 Mix together all the ingredients for the tartare sauce. To make the mushy peas, heat the oil in a small pan, add the onions and garlic and cook gently for 6–7 minutes, until soft and translucent. Add the cream and cook until slightly thickened. Add the peas

and stir well to combine. Blend with a stick blender, until the desired texture is achieved, check the seasoning and add some mint if you fancy it.

8 Heat the oil to 180ºC/350ºF in a deep-fryer or large, heavy pan suitable for deep-frying. Test whether it is ready by putting a piece of bread in the oil. If it spits and fizzes, the oil is ready. Preheat the oven to 110ºC/225ºF/Gas ¼.

9 Blot the fish dry with kitchen paper. Put the remaining flour on a large plate or shallow dish. Working with one fillet at a time, dredge the fillets through the flour, then dip them in the batter to coat completely. Carefully lower the fish into the hot oil and cook for 5–6 minutes or until it starts to float. To get extra crispy shards or bits, spoon a little of the batter over the fish as it cooks.

10 Carefully remove the fish from the hot oil, season with salt and place on a rack in the warm oven. Leave for 5–10 minutes to dry off while you cook the remaining fish in the same way.

11 While the fried fish is resting in the oven, preheat the oil to 180ºC/350ºF in the deep-fryer or large, heavy pan. Lower in the chips in small batches and cook for 5–6 minutes, until golden and crisp. Drain on kitchen paper.

12 Serve the fish with the freshly cooked chips, mushy peas bread and butter, salt, lots of vinegar, lemon wedges and the tartare sauce.

Fish tacos

DIFFICULTY:

EQUIPMENT: Barbecue with a lid, mini food processor

SERVES: 4-6

PREP TIME: 25 minutes, plus preparing the barbecue

COOKING TIME: 15-20 minutes

For that authentic Mexican flavour you could try to go for a warm-water fish such as red snapper, as here, but really any sustainable fish will also do. I've opted for red snapper as it has a meaty firmness that can withstand the searing heat of a barbecue. Nopales add an interesting and authentic touch to these squidgily scrumptious tacos, which are packed with taste-bud tingling textures and flavours. The leaves or pads of the prickly pear plant, which have been removed and preserved in brine, nopales have a texture similar to green beans and an unusual fresh tartness that complements the fish. Be organised with all the toppings and fillings for this recipe, as when the fish is ready it won't wait!

750g/1lb 11oz boneless red snapper fillet, in 1 whole fillet if possible

2.5ml/½ tsp dried oregano

juice of 1 lime

olive oil

FOR THE PICKLED ONIONS

2 red onions, peeled and thinly sliced or cut in wedges

45ml/3 tbsp sherry vinegar

45ml/3 tbsp red wine vinegar

pinch of sugar

FOR THE AVOCADO

2 ripe avocados, peeled, stoned and sliced

pinch of ancho chilli flakes

juice of 1 large lime

salt and ground black pepper

TO SERVE

1 small cos lettuce, leaves picked and washed

nopales, drained and chopped

pico de gallo (see page 82) – this can be as chunky or fine as you like

sour cream

8 fresh corn tortillas

1 Prepare your barbecue to medium hot, so there are glowing coals but no big flames.

2 Prepare the pickled onions by putting all of the ingredients in a pan. Bring to a simmer and cook for about 10 minutes, until the onions are softened. Remove from the heat, transfer to a bowl and leave to cool in the liquid. Drain when cool and set aside.

3 To make the avocado, toss the avocados, chilli flakes, lime and seasoning in a little bowl and set aside.

4 When the barbecue and the other elements are ready, season the fish with oregano, lime juice and olive oil. Place the fish skin side down on the hot grill (broiler) rack, pop the lid on a cook for 5–6 minutes or until the flesh is firm but still slightly opaque. Remove from the grill carefully, place on a plate and keep warm.

5 Set out the onions, avocado, lettuce, nopales, pico de gallo and sour cream. Warm the tortillas in a dry pan or on the barbecue for about 20 seconds. Break the fish flesh into bite-sized flakes.

6 To assemble, lay the warmed tortillas on a board and let diners mix and match ingredients as they please.

VARIATION

Nopales should be available at online food stores and specialist Mexican stores, but if you can't find them then try some shredded green beans instead.

Fried chicken

DIFFICULTY: 🍳🍳

EQUIPMENT: Deep-fryer with a frying basket or a large, heavy pan suitable for deep-frying

SERVES: 4

PREP TIME: 10 minutes, plus 1 hour marinating

COOKING TIME: 30-45 minutes

Possibly originating in the Deep South of the USA, there are many interpretations of fried chicken and argument rages about how to cook it, what seasonings to use, whether you need to marinate it in buttermilk and if you should serve it with biscuits and gravy. It seems that the only thing everyone can agree on is that these irresistibly savoury bites should be eaten with your fingers. One of KFC's great secrets is that they use a low-temperature drying box to drain the chicken after it has been cooked, which ensures that the crispy coating on the outside stays crunchy, while the inside becomes more and more juicy. Get frying.

400ml/14fl oz/1²/₃ cups buttermilk

8 or 9 pieces of chicken, including large drumsticks, thighs, breasts and wings, cut to roughly the same size

250g/9oz/generous 2 cups plain (all-purpose) flour

5ml/1 tsp each of lemon pepper, onion powder, garlic powder, dried thyme, ground white pepper and sweet paprika

7.5ml/1½ tsp cayenne pepper

15ml/1 tbsp salt

oil, for deep-frying

cooked corn on the cob and sauces of your choice, to serve

1 Put the buttermilk and chicken pieces in a large bowl and use your hands to make sure the chicken is coated. Cover and set aside in the fridge for 1 hour.

2 Combine all the dry ingredients in a separate large bowl.

3 When you're ready to cook, heat the oil to 150°C/300°F in a deep-fryer or large, heavy pan suitable for deep-frying. Preheat the oven to 120°C/250°F/Gas ½.

4 Dredge the chicken pieces through the flour mixture, making sure they are coated. Put the chicken into the fryer's metal basket or a bowl and agitate to create rough edges that will crisp up beautifully.

5 Dip the chicken into the warm oil and cook for about 15 minutes, until the skin is crispy and golden. You may need to work in batches; avoid overcrowding the pan.

6 Drain and transfer the chicken to a cooling rack set over a large baking sheet. Place the chicken into the warmed oven and allow to dry and crisp up for about 15 minutes, then serve with the corn and whichever sauces you like.

Jerk chicken with rice & peas

12 boneless chicken thighs, skinned

2 bay leaves

salt and ground black pepper

FOR THE MARINADE

5 garlic cloves, peeled

2 red onions, peeled and roughly chopped

3 fresh Scotch bonnet chillies, halved and seeded

30ml/2 tbsp dark muscovado sugar

30ml/2 tbsp fresh thyme leaves

2.5ml/¹⁄₂ tsp each of crushed allspice berries, ground cinnamon and mixed peppercorns

1.25ml/¹⁄₄ tsp each of grated nutmeg and ground cloves

100ml/3¹⁄₂fl oz/scant ¹⁄₂ cup malt vinegar

30ml/2 tbsp soy sauce

4 spring onions (scallions), green tops finely chopped

45ml/3 tbsp dark rum

salt and ground black pepper

FOR THE RICE AND PEAS

250g/9oz/1¹⁄₄ cups long grain rice, well rinsed

2 x 400g/14oz cans of coconut milk

1 x 400g/14oz can of pigeon peas, drained and rinsed

salt and ground black pepper

TO SERVE

finely chopped green (bell) peppers

lime wedges

Hot Sauce (see page 130

VARIATIONS

• This marinade works really well on home-cooked hams, whole baked fish and prawns (shrimp).
• It is up to you how much chilli you want to use – I feel 3 Scotch bonnets is a good middle ground.

A special aroma of smoky, spicy barbecued chicken fills the air of West London every year as people descend over the bank holiday for the annual Notting Hill carnival – a celebration of Caribbean culture that involves dancing, drinking and eating amazing food. This recipe may seem to use a lot of allspice, Scotch bonnet chilli and onion, but don't be too alarmed by the quantities as cooking the chicken over hot coals reduces that intensity of flavour somewhat. Here, the marinade is a wet one rather than being the dry rub of some recipes. There as many Jamaican jerk chicken recipes as there are oil drum barbecues to cook them on.

DIFFICULTY:

EQUIPMENT: Food processor or mortar and pestle, large lidded container, barbecue

SERVES: 4–6

PREP TIME: 20 minutes, plus 6 hours marinating

COOKING TIME: 30 minutes

1 To make the marinade, put the garlic, onions and Scotch bonnets in a food processor. Blitz to a paste, add the remaining ingredients and season well with salt and pepper. If you don't have a food processor you could use a mortar and pestle.

2 Trim any excess skin or fat from the chicken, place it in a container and add the marinade and the bay leaves. Stir to combine, then put a lid on it and leave it to marinate for 6 hours or overnight.

3 When you are ready, prepare your barbecue to medium hot, so there are glowing coals but no big flames.

4 While the barbecue is heating, make the rice and peas. Put the rice and coconut milk in a pan and cook for 10–15 minutes or until the rice is tender. Stir in the rinsed pigeon peas, season to taste and keep warm until ready to serve.

5 Place the chicken on the barbecue rack skin side down and grill for 8–10 minutes, until crisp on one side. Turn and continue cooking until cooked through and crisp all over – about another 8–10 minutes. Season well with salt and pepper.

6 Serve the chicken with the rice and peas, peppers, lime and some extra hot sauce if you like it spicy.

Chicken tikka masala

8 boneless chicken thighs, skinned and cut in half

cooked basmati rice and warm Naan (see page 129), to serve

FOR THE MARINADE

2 small fresh green chillies, chopped

6 garlic cloves, peeled and crushed

10ml/2 tsp coriander seeds, dry-roasted and crushed

5ml/1 tsp ground turmeric

1 thumb-sized piece of fresh root ginger, peeled and grated

400g/14oz/1¾ cups extra-thick Greek (US strained plain) yogurt

large pinch of salt

10 black peppercorns, crushed

grated rind and juice of 1 lemon

FOR THE MASALA SAUCE

5ml/1 tsp cumin seeds

15ml/1 tbsp coriander seeds

45ml/3 tbsp ghee

2 red onions, peeled and finely sliced

1 thumb-sized piece of fresh root ginger, peeled and grated

5 garlic cloves, peeled and crushed

4 fresh green chillies, 2 trimmed and sliced and 2 split lengthways (seeded if preferred)

5ml/1 tsp garam masala

30ml/2 tbsp tomato paste

600g/1lb 6oz plum tomatoes, chopped, or canned chopped tomatoes

1 chicken stock (bouillon) cube

2 x 400ml/14oz cans coconut milk

salt and ground black pepper

COOK'S TIP

Ghee is clarified butter, with the salt and water removed so that it can withstand high temperatures without burning. It has a wonderful nutty flavour, and a longer shelf life than standard butter.

This Anglo-Indian favourite involves succulent, flame-cooked pieces of marinated chicken bathed in a delicious sweet tomato sauce, and allegedly came into existence when an overworked chef ingeniously (or not) added a can of tomato soup to bulk out a dry sauce. Now a takeaway mainstay and national treasure. There are numerous reasons why homemade is best, from being able to control the levels of heat and salt to using better, fresher ingredients, and tailoring the recipe to suit your tastes. Serve with garlicky, buttery naan or, if time is against you, just serve it with fluffy, aromatic basmati rice.

DIFFICULTY:

EQUIPMENT: Mortar and pestle or mini food processor, long metal skewers, stick blender or blender

SERVES: 4

PREP TIME: 30 minutes, plus 3-4 hours marinating

COOKING TIME: 45 minutes

1 Prepare the marinade by mixing all the ingredients together in a large bowl. Add the chicken, stir to combine well, then cover and leave to marinate for 3–4 hours or overnight.

2 Meanwhile, make the masala sauce. Heat a large, heavy pan over a medium heat. Add the cumin and coriander seeds and toast for about a minute to release the aromas. Finely crush them with a mortar and pestle or whizz them in a mini food processor and set aside.

3 Put the ghee in the warm pan, then add the onions and cook for about 10 minutes, until tinged around the edges and slightly softened. Season with a little salt, add the ginger and garlic and cook for another couple of minutes without colouring. Add the chillies, crushed spices and the garam masala, cook for 30 seconds, then stir in the tomato paste.

4 Tip in the chopped tomatoes and stock and cook, uncovered, for 10–15 minutes, until the tomatoes are squished and pulpy. Season with a little salt and pepper.

5 Add the coconut milk and bring to a simmer, then add the split chillies and cook for 15–20 minutes, until reduced and thickened.

6 Meanwhile, preheat the grill (broiler) to high. Thread the marinated chicken on to metal skewers and place these on to a grill tray. Cook for 6–7 minutes on each side, until cooked through and slightly charred.

7 Taste the sauce and adjust the seasoning as necessary. Remove the split chillies and blend the sauce until smooth with a stick blender or in a blender.

8 Serve the chicken pieces with some sauce ladled over, accompanied by some basmati rice and warm naan breads.

assaman curry

Massaman is a fiery Thai curry with many cross-cultural culinary influences from Malaysia and India. Laden with fresh aromatic spices that give heat and balance, it's a bowlful of goodness that seems to nourish and heal body and soul and is one of the top choices at takeaways. In this version we use beef – look for the cuts suitable for slow-cooking, such as shin or brisket. The base of the dish is its paste, which is spiked with chillies and tingly lemongrass and galangal. You could buy it ready-made from Asian supermarkets or online, but making your own tastes better and allows you to tinker to suit your palate: more or less chilli? more lime? more shrimp paste?

30ml/2 tbsp oil

0g/1lb 11oz chuck steak, shin or
t, cut into large bite-sized cubes

l/17fl oz/generous 2 cups good-
quality beef stock

5ml/1 tbsp tamarind paste (made
ording to the packet instructions)

large waxy potatoes, peeled and
chopped into large chunks

small bunch of fresh Thai basil

1 cinnamon stick, snapped

400ml/14oz can of coconut milk

Thai fish sauce, to taste

salt and ground black pepper

FOR THE PASTE

15ml/1 tbsp coriander seeds

5ml/1 tsp cumin seeds

3 cloves, crushed

1 star anise

5 cardamom pods

l/1 tsp white peppercorns

of freshly grated nutmeg

ots, peeled and roughly
chopped

garlic cloves, peeled

lks, roughly chopped

sh galangal, peeled
d roughly chopped

s, stalks trimmed

sp shrimp paste

pinch of salt

TO SERVE

smine rice

chopped

wedges

DIFFICULTY:

EQUIPMENT: Mortar and pestle or mini food processor, large flameproof casserole with a tight-fitting lid

SERVES: 4–5

PREP TIME: 20 minutes

COOKING TIME: 1–1½ hours

1 To make the paste, toast the seeds, cloves, star anise, cardamom and peppercorns in a dry pan for 2–3 minutes, until fragrant. Use a mortar and pestle or mini food processor and pound or blitz to a powder. Add the remaining ingredients and blend until a smooth paste has formed.

2 Preheat the oven to 120°C/250°F/ Gas ½.

3 Heat the oil over a medium heat in a large flameproof casserole with a tight-fitting lid. Add the beef to the pan and brown it on all sides.

4 Stir in 75ml/5 tbsp of the paste and allow it to mingle with the beef. Season with a little salt and pepper, add the beef stock and bring to a simmer.

5 Add the tamarind paste, potatoes, basil, cinnamon and coconut milk. Pop the lid on and cook in the oven for about 1½ hours, until the meat has a bit of give in it, removing the lid for the last 20 minutes so the sauce can reduce a little and to concentrate the flavours.

6 About 20 minutes before serving, cook the jasmine rice according to packet instructions, until tender and sticky.

7 Remove the curry from the oven and add a little fish sauce to taste. Serve with the sticky jasmine rice, chopped peanuts and lime wedges.

COOK'S TIP
The paste can be made well in advance and stored in an airtight container or screw-top jar in the fridge for up to 5 days.

Deep-dish cheese & pepperoni pizza

Fast food deep-dish pizza has a reputation for being low-quality, when it's made properly it's one of the tastiest of all pizzas. Loac with a simple cheese and tomato topping, there are endless opti when it comes to enhancing the satisfying crisp crust, which ca brushed with garlic or stuffed with mozzarella. The ingredients simple, but by using the best-quality flour for the base and maki your own intense tomato sauce you're guaranteed a taste sensa that can't be matched by the stodgy offerings that you can buy.

FOR THE TOMATO SAUCE

30ml/2 tbsp olive oil

5 garlic cloves, peeled and finely crushed

5ml/1 tsp oregano

4 x 400g/14oz cans plum tomatoes, crushed with a potato masher

pinch of sugar

salt and ground black pepper

FOR THE DOUGH

10ml/2 tsp dried active yeast

375ml/13fl oz/scant 1½ cups water

pinch of sugar

600g/1lb 6oz/5¼ cups 00 flour, or strong white bread flour

large pinch of salt

butter, for greasing

semolina, for sprinkling

FOR THE TOPPING

200g/7oz/scant 2 cups grated mozzarella cheese

75g/3oz sliced pepperoni or salami

100ml/3½fl oz/scant ½ cup olive oil

2 garlic cloves, peeled and crushed

15ml/1 tbsp chopped rosemary

45ml/3 tbsp butter, melted

dried chilli flakes, plus extra to serve

salt and ground black pepper

ground Parmesan, to serve

COOK'S TIP

There are lots of different types of bread and pizza flours on the market with various grades. Type 00 is an Italian flour used for pasta and Italian breads. Read the packet to make sure it's suitable for pizza. Ordinary strong white bread flour will be fine.

DIFFICULTY: 🍳🍳

EQUIPMENT: Large pan with a tight-fitting lid, stick blender or blender, heavy tin (pan), ovenproof skillet or pizza stone

MAKES: 4–5 pizzas

PREP TIME: 40 minutes, plus 1½ hours proving

COOKING TIME: 12 minutes for the sauce, 8–12 minutes per pizza

---

1 First, prepare the tomato sauce. Heat the oil in a large pan with a tight-fitting lid over a low heat. Add the garlic and oregano, cook for a minute, then add the tomatoes. Bring to a simmer, then pop the lid on and cook for about 10 minutes, until the tomatoes are soft and pulpy.

2 Season with sugar, salt and pepper, then blend with a stick blender or in a blender until smooth. Set aside to cool. You will have more than enough, so freeze the surplus in small containers for future pizzas parties.

3 To make the dough, put the in a small bowl with 75ml/ of the water and a pinch of sug to dissolve, then set aside son warm to activate for about 1C until frothy.

4 Mix the flour and salt ir bowl. Make a well in th mix in the water and yeas

5 Use your hands to mixture together in tip it on to a lightly flo knead for about 10 m dough is smooth an It should bounce b gently prodded.

6 Grease the dough, cov towel and lea until double

7 Knock doug five equ one of put th yeas ess yc c

8 Generously grease the inside of a heavy tin (pan), ovenproof skillet or pizza stone. Sprinkle with a little semolina to give it that crispy base (trade secret), then roll the ball of dough you've kept out into a small, reasonably thick (about 2.5cm/1in) disc. Put the dough disc in the tin or skillet or on the pizza stone and leave it to prove for about 30 minutes, until doubled in size. Preheat the oven to 220ºC/425ºF/Gas 7.

9 When the dough is ready, gently spread a little of the cold tomato sauce over the base, leaving a rim of about 1cm/¹⁄₂in around the edge. Sprinkle with some of the grated cheese and top with pepperoni or salami. Drizzle with a little olive oil and season with salt and pepper.

10 Bake for 10–12 minutes, until the edge is golden and the pizza is well risen.

11 Meanwhile, mash the garlic, rosemary and butter together, then brush some of the mixture over the crust of the cooked pizza. Sprinkle with crushed chillies.

12 Slice the pizza and watch that cheese stretch. Serve with ground Parmesan and extra chilli flakes on the side.

DIFFICULTY:

EQUIPMENT: Pizza stone or heavy baking tray, pizza peel or a thin, large board

SERVES: 4

PREP TIME: 30 minutes, plus at least 50 minutes proving

COOKING TIME: 3-4 minutes per pizza

FOR THE DOUGH

600g/1lb 5oz/5¼ cups strong 00 flour or strong white bread flour, plus a little extra for dusting

15ml/1 tbsp salt

30ml/2 tbsp olive oil, plus extra for greasing

10g/¼oz easy-blend (rapid-rise) dried yeast

350ml/12fl oz/1½ cups blood-warm water

polenta or cornmeal, for sprinkling

FOR THE TOPPING

Tomato Sauce (see page 98)

200g/7oz baby spinach leaves

200g/7oz mozzarella, shredded

250g/9oz mushrooms (porcini or field (portobello) mushrooms if available), sliced

115g/4oz Gorgonzola picante cheese

olive oil

flaky sea salt and ground black pepper

Thin-crust Neapolitan pizza

No matter how amazing it was when it came out of the oven, takeaway pizza is never great because it inevitably steams in the box, making it soggy and unappetising by the time you eat it. Fortunately, it's fairly easy to make at home, especially if you invest in a pizza stone, which allows the base to cook to a crisp finish while the convection heat cooks the sides and topping. If you are lucky enough to have a wood-fired oven then you'll be able to achieve near-Neapolitan pizza perfection: chewy crust, crispy charred base, just a few flavoursome toppings that work in harmony with rather than drowning out the beautiful base... Buon appetito!

Prepare the dough by mixing the flour, salt, oil and yeast together in a large bowl or an electric mixer with a dough hook attached.

Make a well in the middle and add the water, mixing to form a soft, sticky dough. Tip on to a lightly floured surface and knead for 8–10 minutes by hand, or use the dough hook for 5 minutes, to form a smooth and satisfying silky dough.

Oil the inside of the bowl and return the dough to it to prove. At this stage you can place the dough in the fridge for it to slow-prove over about 24 hours, or leave it in warm place to develop for about 50 minutes–1½ hours, depending on the room temperature. The dough should have risen and developed air bubbles below the surface and be about twice its original size by the time it is ready.

Put the pizza stone or heavy baking tray in the oven and whack it up to full heat. A little trick to get your stone or tray super hot is to also turn the grill (broiler) on, if it's in the main body of the oven, to boost the temperature of the stone. Turn off the grill before using the oven.

Knock back (punch down) the dough in the bowl with your fist, then divide it into four balls. Work with one ball at a time and store the remaining ones in the fridge on a large dinner plate.

From here on everything needs to be organised as you have to work quickly! Roll the dough out on a lightly floured surface to about 25–30cm/10–12in in diameter – be daring and make it as thin as you can, it doesn't have to be a perfect circle.

Sprinkle some of the polenta on to the pizza peel, then carefully lift and lay your pizza base on top. Tidy any of the edges so everything is flat.

Dollop a couple of generous tablespoons of tomato sauce in the middle and gently spread it around with the back of the spoon. Add the remaining toppings, starting with the spinach leaves and finishing with the mushrooms and Gorgonzola. Sprinkle with a little sea salt and pepper and drizzle generously with your most treasured olive oil.

As swiftly and confidently as you can, slide the prepared pizza on to the pizza stone. The first one is the trickiest. Bake until the pizza is cooked. Peek under the base from time to time – you are looking for a crispy base with melted cheese and slightly charred mushrooms on the top.

Remove with the peel (again with confidence) and place on a cutting board. Repeat with the remaining dough balls and toppings. Slice and serve.

COOK'S TIP
The polenta plays two roles: first, it makes the base crispy; second, the grains act as little wheels that help you slide your prepared pizza on to the pizza stone.

VARIATION
If you want to try something different, try roasting a whole butternut squash in the oven until tender. Remove the skin and pips and blend to a purée, then use it in place of the tomato sauce. It makes a delicious, sweet and smooth alternative.

Nasi goreng

DIFFICULTY: 🍳

SPECIAL EQUIPMENT: Wok or large, heavy frying pan

SERVES: 2

PREP TIME: 20 minutes

COOKING TIME: 30 minutes

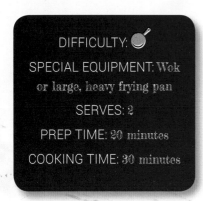

Indonesia was once at the epicentre of the global spice trade, with spices, tea and coffee being traded from Jakarta to many European countries. Little wonder, then, that spices are such a feature of the country's cuisine, and where better to showcase them than Indonesia's national rice dish. Meaning 'fried rice', nasi goreng is eaten at any time of the day and there are as many versions of it as there are cooks in Indonesia. It's the perfect way to use up any leftover rice. The only hard-and-fast rules are that the rice should be cool and the grains separated before it is fried, and that it is served with an egg on top, though how this is cooked is down to personal preference – I like it to have a crispy white skirt and a runny yolk, but it's entirely up to you.

200g/7oz/1 cup basmati rice
30ml/2 tbsp oil, for frying
5 Asian shallots, peeled and finely sliced
4 garlic cloves, peeled and crushed
15ml/1 tbsp shrimp paste
15ml/1 tbsp grated fresh root ginger
2 fresh bird's-eye chillies, thinly sliced
2 carrots, peeled and cut into matchsticks
15ml/1 tbsp tomato paste
30ml/2 tbsp kecap manis
2 eggs
salt and ground black pepper

TO SERVE

2 spring onions (scallions), sliced thinly
Hot Sauce (see page 130)
sliced cucumber
chilli threads

VARIATION

If you can't find kecap manis – Indonesian sweet soy sauce – then you can just mix a little regular dark soy sauce with some honey.

1 Cook the basmati according to packet instructions, then leave to cool completely.

2 Heat 5ml/1 tsp of the oil in a wok or large, heavy frying pan. Add the shallots and a pinch of salt and cook for 5–6 minutes, until wilted and starting to crisp up. Remove from the pan with a slotted spoon and drain on kitchen paper.

3 Heat 15ml/1 tbsp of the oil in the pan over a medium heat. Add the garlic, shrimp paste, ginger and chillies. Cook for 2–3 minutes, moving it around.

4 Add the carrots and stir-fry for 2 minutes, then stir in the tomato paste and kecap manis and cook for 2–3 minutes.

5 Add the rice, making sure that all the grains are nicely separated. Cook, stirring, for 5–6 minutes, until heated through and the grains are well coated.

6 Meanwhile, put the remaining oil in a small frying pan and place over a high heat. When the oil is super hot, carefully crack in an egg and allow it to cook until a little frilly crispy edge has formed. Remove and drain on kitchen paper. Repeat with the other egg.

7 Mound the rice on to warm plates and lay an egg on each portion. Top with spring onions, hot sauce, sliced cucumber, crispy shallots and chilli threads.

Vietnamese pho

DIFFICULTY:
EQUIPMENT: N/a
SERVES: 4-6
PREP TIME: 25 minutes
COOKING TIME: 1 hour

Probably the best pot noodle known to man. Much like ramen, pho requires a really rich, concentrated bone broth. You can make a dark one from beef bones, but the recipe given here is for a lighter version made from chicken bones, wings and wing tips. To this elixir are added a cornucopia of aromatic Asian ingredients that leave the broth in a state of harmony with a perfect balance of salty, sweet, sour and spicy notes. All that's needed now are poached chicken thighs, noodles and bean sprouts for substance and the tastiest bowl of goodness possible is ready for slurping.

about 1kg/2¼lb chicken carcasses, wings and wing tips

6 boneless chicken thighs, skinned

5 cloves

2 star anise

2 bay leaves

7.5cm/3in piece of galangal, peeled and sliced

7.5cm/3in piece of fresh root ginger, peeled and sliced

½ head of garlic, bashed

2 lemongrass stalks, sliced

45ml/3 tbsp light soy sauce

15ml/1 tbsp Thai fish sauce

15ml/1 tbsp sugar

lime juice, to taste

400g/14oz rice noodles (ban pho)

lime wedges, to serve

FOR THE GARNISHES

large bunch of fresh mint

small bunch of fresh coriander (cilantro)

small bunch of fresh holy basil

3 fresh bird's-eye chillies, sliced

4 spring onions (scallions), trimmed and sliced into long, thin ribbons

50g/2oz/¼ cup bean sprouts, trimmed

1 To make the stock, put the chicken carcasses and wings into a large stockpot and cover completely with about 2.4 litres/4 pints/10 cups cold water. Slowly bring up to the boil and simmer for about 30 minutes. As it boils you will notice cloudy impurities rising to the surface. Skim these away and discard.

2 Remove the chicken carcasses and pass the stock through a sieve into a clean pan. Add the chicken thighs, cloves, star anise, bay leaves, galangal, ginger, garlic, lemongrass and soy sauce.

3 Simmer gently for about 20–25 minutes, until the chicken is cooked. Remove the chicken, shred it finely with a couple of forks and set aside. Pass the stock once more through a sieve. Add the fish sauce to taste and balance with a little sugar and lime juice.

4 Prepare the noodles according to the packet instructions, then divide between four warmed bowls.

5 Ladle over some of the hot broth and then let diners add their own garnishes. Serve with extra lime wedges.

COOK'S TIP
Make your stock as clear as possible by putting the bones in cold water before bringing them up to the boil. This will draw all the impurities to the surface, where they can be skimmed off, giving you, ultimately, a clear and rich stock.

Chicken katsu curry

FOR THE KOMBU (KELP) STOCK

1 kombu (kelp) sheet, soaked in cold water for 2–3 hours

400ml/14fl oz/1²/₃ cups chicken stock

FOR THE CHICKEN

2 large chicken breasts, skinned and trimmed

90g/3¹/₂oz/³/₄ cup plain (all-purpose) flour

2 eggs, beaten

115g/4oz/2 cups panko breadcrumbs

oil, for frying

salt and ground black pepper

FOR THE CURRY SAUCE

15ml/1 tbsp oil

2 onions, peeled and finely chopped

2 garlic cloves, peeled and crushed

5cm/2in piece of fresh root ginger, peeled and grated

5ml/1 tsp medium curry powder

2.5ml/¹/₂ tsp garam masala

15ml/1 tbsp plain (all-purpose) flour

2 small waxy potatoes, peeled and cubed

2 carrots, peeled and cubed

400ml/14fl oz/1²/₃ cups kombu dashi

15ml/1 tbsp each of light soy sauce, rice vinegar and mango chutney

5ml/1 tsp honey

FOR THE CARROT PICKLE

1 large carrot, peeled and cut into matchsticks

5ml/1 tsp rice vinegar

2.5ml/¹/₂ tsp sugar

salt and ground black pepper

TO SERVE

150g/5oz/³/₄ cup Japanese sticky rice, cooked according to packet instructions

Japanese pickles

spring onions (scallions), trimmed and sliced

The origins of this dish are slightly unusual. In Japan it is seen as western, but in the west it is seen as Japanese. It is rumoured to have been brought to Japan by the British, probably via India. It's a comfort food dish that works very well with chicken, pork, or tofu, bathed in a rich curry sauce and contrasted with a side of delicious pickled vegetables. Panko breadcrumbs provide a light and crunchy coating for the fried chicken in this version, and its this freshness and crunch that can so easily be lost in takeaway versions, which steam en route.

DIFFICULTY:

EQUIPMENT: Deep-fryer or a large, heavy pan suitable for deep-frying

SERVES: 2

PREP TIME: 30 minutes, plus 2–3 hours soaking

COOKING TIME: 45 minutes

1 First, make the kombu stock by putting the soaked kombu in a pan with the stock and simmering for 15–20 minutes. Remove from the heat and discard the kombu. Chill for up to 5 days or freeze for up to 3 months.

2 To prepare the chicken, slice the breasts in half horizontally – this will give you an even cooking area.

3 Put the flour, eggs and breadcrumbs on to three separate dinner plates. Season the flour and eggs with a little salt and pepper.

4 Dredge one of the chicken pieces into the flour, shake off any excess and plunge it into the egg. Transfer it to the breadcrumbs and turn it, patting the crumbs on until it is completely covered. Set aside on a wire rack.

5 Repeat with the other chicken pieces and set aside.

6 To make the curry sauce, heat the oil in a medium pan over a medium heat. Add the onions and a little salt and cook for 5–6 minutes, until tender and translucent. Add the garlic and ginger and cook for a minute, then stir in the powdered spices, flour, potatoes and carrots and cook for another minute. Add the kombu dashi and simmer until the vegetables are tender to the bite – about 10 minutes. Add the soy sauce, vinegar, mango chutney and honey, then season with a little pepper. Set aside and keep warm.

7 To make the carrot pickle, mix everything together. Heat the oil for the chicken to 180°C/350°F in a deep-fryer or deep, heavy pan suitable for deep-frying.

8 Lower the chicken pieces into the hot oil and cook for about 5–6 minutes, until golden and they start to float in the oil. Remove and drain on kitchen paper, then slice.

9 Put some cooked sticky rice in the bottom of two bowls, top with some of the curry sauce and then the chicken. Serve with the pickled carrots, Japanese pickles and spring onions.

Sweet-and-sour pork

The popularity of sweet-and-sour dishes knows no bounds, yet in reality what arrives on the back of a bike often disappoints. The aim of this recipe is to raise the bar and give you a taste sensation that a takeaway simply can't deliver. What's more, it's such an easy dish to put together, requiring just a little gentle pottering to make a perfectly seasoned sauce then a quick flash-fry of some top-quality meat. Then all you have to do is combine the two with noodles or egg-fried rice, as you prefer, and voilà, the perfect sweet-and-sour dish in less time than it takes to place your order and pace about waiting to be underwhelmed once it arrives.

DIFFICULTY:

EQUIPMENT: Large wok or large, heavy frying pan

SERVES: 4

PREP TIME: 15 minutes

COOKING TIME: 15 minutes

30ml/2 tbsp oil, for frying, plus extra for deep-frying

1 carrot, peeled and sliced into matchsticks

2 red onions, peeled and thinly sliced

1 red and 1 green (bell) pepper, seeded and cut into large cubes

2 garlic cloves, peeled and crushed

thumb-sized piece of fresh root ginger, peeled and finely grated

2 eggs, lightly beaten

45ml/3 tbsp cornflour (cornstarch)

600g/1lb 6oz pork fillet (tenderloin), trimmed and cut into bite-sized pieces

salt and ground black pepper

egg-fried rice (see page 110) or cooked noodles, to serve

small bunch of spring onions (scallions), chopped, to garnish

FOR THE SWEET-AND-SOUR SAUCE

100ml/3½fl oz/scant ½ cup rice wine vinegar

200ml/7fl oz/scant 1 cup white wine vinegar

200g/7oz/scant 1 cup muscovado (molasses) sugar

30ml/2 tsp light soy sauce

5ml/1 tsp mustard powder

1 small pineapple, peeled, cored and cubed

1 First, make the sweet-and-sour sauce by putting the vinegars, sugar, soy sauce and mustard powder in a medium pan. Stir over a low heat to dissolve the sugar. Increase the heat and cook for 8–10 minutes, until thick and syrupy, then add the pineapple and set aside.

2 Heat 30ml/2 tbsp of the oil in a large wok or heavy frying pan, add the carrot, onion and peppers and stir-fry for a minute, until slightly softened. Add the garlic and ginger and stir-fry for another minute, until fragrant. Cover and keep warm.

3 Heat the remaining oil in a large wok or heavy frying pan.

4 Put the beaten egg in one dish and the cornflour in another. Coat the pork with the egg and then dredge it through the cornflour. Dust off any excess and add the pork in small batches to the hot oil. Fry for 3–4 minutes, until crispy. Drain on kitchen paper and cook the remaining pork.

5 Add the pork to the sweet-and-sour sauce along with the carrot and pepper mixture. Serve with egg-fried rice or steamed noodles, garnished with spring onions.

Sichuan pork

DIFFICULTY: 🍳

EQUIPMENT: Wok or large, heavy frying pan

SERVES: 2

PREP TIME: 10 minutes

COOKING TIME: 20 minutes

Sichuan food is renowned for being hot and spicy. This is little surprise, given that both fresh chillies – especially those known as 'facing heaven' chillies, so called because they grow upwards – and the eponymous Sichuan peppercorns feature heavily in the region's dishes, as here. Fillet of pork is particularly suitable for quick stir-fried dishes, ask your butcher to trim the silvery sinew that is at the head end (thick end) of the fillet as this may leave the meat slightly tough, or give it a whirl yourself with the point of a short, sharp knife. You don't have to be a slave to authenticity but good chilli powder will not only give you the desired fiery heat but will have a little sweetness to it too, which will balance the dish.

450g/1lb pork fillet (tenderloin), trimmed and sliced into 7.5cm/3in slices

about 15ml/1 tbsp light soy sauce

15ml/1 tbsp rice wine or very dry sherry

about 7.5ml/1½ tsp sesame oil

30ml/2 tbsp oil, for frying

5ml/1 tsp Sichuan peppercorns, lightly crushed

3 garlic cloves, peeled and crushed

pinch each of sugar and salt

2 green (bell) peppers, seeded and sliced

3 medium fresh red chillies, bullet style or facing heaven if available, trimmed and sliced

FOR THE EGG-FRIED RICE

100g/4oz/½ cup long grain rice

5ml/1 tsp oil

2 eggs, beaten

115g/4oz/1 cup frozen peas, thawed

salt and ground black pepper

1 Start by making the egg-fried rice. Put the rice in a pan and cook according to packet instructions. Set aside.

2 Meanwhile, make the stir-fry. Combine the sliced pork, soy sauce, rice wine or sherry, and sesame oil in a bowl.

3 Heat 15ml/1 tbsp of the oil in a large wok or heavy frying pan over a medium heat. When it's smoking hot, carefully add the pork (it will spit at you) and stir-fry for about a minute, until just sealed. Tip the pork and its juices out of the wok and set aside. Keep the wok on the heat.

4 Add another 15ml/1 tbsp of the oil to the wok and swirl it round the edges to give a good coating. When it's smoking again, add the peppercorns, garlic, sugar, salt and green peppers and stir-fry for another minute.

5 Add the chillies and stir-fry for 10 seconds. Add a couple of splashes of cold water, return the pork (along with its juices) to the pan and heat the mixture through. Add a touch more soy sauce and sesame oil to suit your taste. Set aside and keep warm.

6 Finish the egg-fried rice by putting a large frying pan over a medium heat. Add the oil and the egg. Let the egg settle on the bottom of the pan, then gently stir to cook it evenly.

7 Add the cooked rice and thawed peas to the pan and stir to combine. You should have little strips of egg through the rice mixture. Season to taste. Serve the warm pork with the egg-fried rice.

Baby back pork ribs

DIFFICULTY: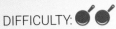

EQUIPMENT: Barbecue, mortar and pestle

SERVES 2-3

PREP TIME: 10 minutes, plus 1 hour marinating

COOKING TIME: 3-4 hours

Sticky spiced sauce, unctuous meat and a mellow deep porky flavour... We can only be talking about a rack of pork ribs – the ultimate finger lickin' good fakeaway feast. The rack of pork ribs itself comes from the head end of the pig, under the pork belly. They need marinating to tenderise them and then long, slow cooking to render the fat and sinew and slowly draw the delicious meat from the bone, but it's all time well spent and requires very little actual work. The only other things you need are an appetite and a finger bowl.

1kg/2¼lb pork ribs (see Cook's Tip)
Home-made Barbecue Sauce (see page 64), to serve

FOR THE RUB

10ml/2 tsp fennel seeds
5ml/1 tsp cumin seeds
15ml/1 tbsp coriander seeds
5ml/1 tsp black peppercorns
30ml/2 tbsp salt
15ml/1 tbsp soft dark brown sugar
5ml/1 tsp smoked paprika
5ml/1 tsp dried oregano
2.5ml/½ tsp dried rosemary

1 Put a frying pan over a medium heat, then add the fennel, cumin and coriander seeds and toast for about 2 minutes, until fragrant. Tip them into a mortar and add the peppercorns, then lightly crush them all with the pestle. Add the remaining rub ingredients and stir to combine.

2 Put the ribs in a roasting tray and press the rub into the flesh, reserving a little for seasoning at the end. Cover and leave to marinate in the fridge for an hour if possible.

3 Prepare a barbecue for indirect cooking on a low heat. Place the ribs on the barbecue rack and cook indirectly on a low heat for 3–4 hours, until the meat has receded a little from the bone and you can see the tips of the ribs. You can also do this in a low oven – about 110°C/225°F/Gas ¼

4 Stoke up the barbecue a little for direct grilling, or preheat a grill (broiler) if you're using the oven. Place the ribs directly over or under the heat and grill (broil) for 2–3 minutes on each side. Smear some of the barbecue sauce all over the ribs and return to the grill for 30 seconds on each side, so the glaze sticks.

5 Remove carefully with tongs and serve immediately with a little of the reserved rub sprinkled on top.

COOK'S TIP

If you are on good terms with your butcher, ask them to remove the sinew layer at the back of the ribs and cut them St Louis style, which involves squaring them up by removing the flap and the sternum.

Pad Thai

DIFFICULTY: 🍳

EQUIPMENT: Wok or large, heavy frying pan

SERVES: 2

PREP TIME: 20 minutes

COOKING TIME: 25 minutes

Takeaway Pad Thai is another dish that suffers dreadfully from the condensation in the container while it is en route to your door. The whole point of this Thai street-food classic is the contrasting crunchy textures of onion, peanuts and bean sprouts against soft noodles and juicy prawns, all bound together by the freshness of lime, chilli and herbs. Given that it's so easy to rustle up yourself, there is really no excuse for settling for the limp offerings that often land on your plate. This is also a great storecupboard standby, as the ingredients can all be stored in the freezer.

200g/7oz dried medium rice noodles (sen lek)

30ml/2 tbsp oil

2 garlic cloves, peeled and crushed

3 Thai shallots, peeled and thinly sliced

400g/14oz raw king prawns (jumbo shrimp), peeled and deveined

15ml/1 tbsp dried prawns (shrimp), rinsed and drained

15ml/1 tbsp Thai fish sauce

2.5ml/½ tsp crushed palm sugar or soft light brown sugar

15ml/1 tbsp tamarind pulp (made according to the packet instructions)

5ml/1 tsp white wine vinegar

2 eggs, lightly beaten

50g/2oz/¼ cup trimmed bean sprouts

3 spring onions (scallions), trimmed and sliced into 2cm/¾in lengths

lime wedges, crushed peanuts and roasted chilli powder, to serve

1 Prepare the noodles according to the packet instructions, then blanch them in a pan of boiling water for 10 seconds, drain and set aside.

2 Put the oil in a large wok or heavy frying pan, and place over a medium heat. Add the garlic and shallots and cook for 3–4 minutes, until golden and fragrant. Add the prawns and stir to combine.

3 Put the dried prawns, fish sauce, sugar, tamarind pulp and vinegar in a bowl and stir until the sugar has dissolved.

4 Add the eggs to the wok, stirring quickly to break them into a rough scramble. Add the noodles and stir a little.

5 Add the tamarind mixture to the wok and stir to combine, then add the beansprouts and spring onions and stir to combine everything well.

6 Serve immediately with lime wedges, crushed peanuts and roasted chilli powder.

COOK'S TIP
Prepared tamarind pulp or paste, also called tamarind 'water', can be bought in most supermarkets. Do follow the packet instructions, as some are more concentrated than others and require a different amount of water.

VARIATION
Using fresh prawns (shrimp) is most traditional, but you could substitute these with shredded cooked chicken or firm slices of fried tofu, if you wish.

Char sui ramen

DIFFICULTY:

EQUIPMENT: Wok or large, heavy frying pan

SERVES: 2

PREP TIME: 30 minutes, plus overnight marinating

COOKING TIME: 2 hours

Ramen first became popular in the west following the introduction of packaged instant ramen, which consist of dried noodles, dry vegetables and seasoning packs that can be rehydrated with boiling water and 5 minutes' loitering. Since then there's been a culinary boom in the fresh type, and the dish appears on menus at all sorts of popular restaurants and, increasingly, in home kitchens. The key to making ramen yourself is organising the ingredients, which in essence consist of: stock, noodles and a prime ingredient such as meat, fish or vegetables. This may sound simple, but quality is crucial – the stock must be flavoursome, the noodles long enough that they don't snap when slurped, and the protein element tender.

about 300g/11oz Char sui pork (see page 62)

200g/7oz ramen noodles

3 baby pak choi (bok choy), trimmed and sliced

Japanese chilli oil

5 spring onions (scallions), trimmed and finely sliced

mixed toasted sesame seeds

selection of Japanese ramen pickles, to serve

FOR THE EGGS

6 large (US extra large) eggs

75ml/5 tbsp dark soy sauce

45ml/3 tbsp mirin

45ml/3 tbsp sugar

FOR THE STOCK

1kg/2¼lb chicken wings or carcasses from past roasts

1 kombu sheet, soaked in cold water

pinch of bonito flakes

75g/3oz fresh root ginger, unpeeled, bashed

5 garlic cloves, unpeeled, bashed

1 First, prepare the eggs by cooking them in boiling water for about 5 minutes. Refresh in ice-cold water, peel and place in a small container. Mix the rest of the ingredients together and pour over the eggs. Drape a sheet of kitchen paper over the eggs, with the ends dangling in the sauce, so the tops of the eggs get an even covering of the soy mixture. Allow to sit overnight.

2 Put the chicken in a large bowl and pour over boiling water to cover. Allow it to sit for 10 minutes, then drain and transfer to a clean pan. Pour in 3 litres/5 pints/12½ cups cold water.

3 Add the rest of the ingredients to the pan, bring to a simmer and cook for 1–1½ hours, skimming off any scum as it rises. When the stock is ready, pass it through a sieve into a large bowl, discard the carcass and bits and set aside.

4 When the pork, eggs and stock are ready, lay out all the other ingredients so everything is at room temperature.

5 Cook the noodles in a large pan of boiling water for 2–3 minutes or according to the instructions on the packet, then drain.

6 Divide the stock among four bowls, add the noodles and a slice or two of the pork. Halve the eggs and place to the side of the bowl, then add the pak choi and sprinkle over the chilli oil, spring onions and sesame seeds. Add whatever pickles take your fancy. Serve hot and slurp fast!

COOK'S TIPS

• If you can get your hands on fresh ramen noodles then use them, but there are very good dried ones available in most supermarkets and Asian stores.

• You will need a small container that will hold the eggs. An old take-away container with a plastic lid is ideal. The longer they sit in the soy and mirin the more flavoursome they will become, so it's worth giving them a little time to bathe to give your ramen real street cred.

Sides and Accompaniments

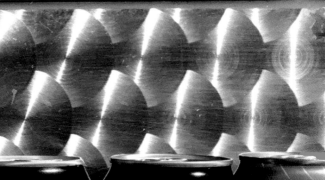

Vegetable pakoras

DIFFICULTY: 🍳🍳

EQUIPMENT: Deep-fryer or large, heavy pan suitable for deep-frying

SERVES: 6

PREP TIME: 20 minutes

COOKING TIME: 3–4 minutes per batch

The simplest of street snacks, pakoras can be found in Pakistan, Afghanistan, India and Bangladesh, where they are enjoyed as a crunchy, savoury appetiser or as a tasty snack to accompany cold beers. The light gram-flour coating around the vegetables should just bind the vegetables – after cooking you should still be able to identify them. What is lost in the takeaway or supermarket container is freshness, resulting in bland, soggy, greasy snacks. Use crisp, fresh vegetables, and eat the pakoras hot and fresh for a completely different experience. Avoid high-water vegetables such as sweet potatoes and aubergines (eggplants). Carrots, onion, cauliflower, broccoli, bell peppers and potatoes all work well.

500g/1¼ lb mixed selection of vegetables, such as peeled carrots, tenderstem cauliflower including leaves, peeled red onions and tenderstem broccoli, all cut into very small pieces

oil, for deep-frying

FOR THE BATTER
190g/6½oz/1⅔ cups gram flour

2.5ml/½ tsp ground turmeric

5ml/1 tsp chilli powder

5ml/1 tsp garam masala

5ml/1 tsp ground cumin

3 fresh green chillies, finely chopped

12 curry leaves

5ml/1 tsp bicarbonate of soda (baking soda)

large pinch of salt

about 350ml/12fl oz/1½ cups water

TO SERVE
pinch of flaky sea salt

Pakora Sauce (see page 132)

Hot Sauce (see page 130)

cold beer (optional)

1 Cut the veg into small dice, or small strips all around the same size.

2 Mix all the batter ingredients together in a large bowl, adding enough water to make a smooth medium batter.

3 Heat the oil to 190°C/375°F in a deep-fryer or large, heavy pan suitable for deep-frying. Test by adding a curry leaf – if it splutters and fizzes, then it's ready.

4 Working in small batches, scoop up tablespoons of the finely chopped vegetable mixture, dip the whole spoon in the batter and then carefully lower into the hot oil. When they float and are golden and crispy they are cooked – about 3–4 minutes.

5 Scoop out the cooked pakoras and drain on kitchen paper. Repeat until all the veg are used up.

6 Serve with a sprinkle of sea salt, cooling Pakora Sauce and a hot sauce too, if you fancy it.

Poppadums

DIFFICULTY:

EQUIPMENT: Mortar and pestle or mini food processor, microwave

SERVES: 4

PREP TIME: 5 minutes

COOKING TIME: 7-8 minutes

The ultimate one-stop meal, the thali — a selection of dishes served on a platter — is popular throughout India. Among the foods that usually feature are poppadums, which are broken into shards and sprinkled over dishes for added crunch or kept whole and used as a cap on a biryani. It is mostly in westernised restaurants that they are served at the beginning of the meal to nibble with drinks and to whet the appetite for the spicy onslaught, and a mighty fine appetiser they make too. This recipe is an easy way to jazz up plain, ready-to cook poppadums and eat them them fresh from the pan at home.

5ml/1 tsp black mustard seeds
5ml/1 tsp coriander seeds
5ml/1 tsp cumin seeds
45ml/3 tbsp mustard oil
5ml/1 tsp chilli flakes
30ml/2 tbsp fresh coriander (cilantro), finely chopped
8 raw poppadums
Indian Chutneys (see page 132), to serve

COOK'S TIP

If you don't have a microwave the poppadums can be fried one by one in 2–4cm vegetable oil, for 2–3 seconds, or follow the instructions on the packet. Instead of brushing the poppadums with spiced oil before frying, sprinkle the dry spice mix over as soon as you remove the poppadum from the pan.

VARIATION

If you want to make plain ones then just brush the poppadums with oil and microwave according to the packet instructions.

1 Put the spices in a frying pan and dry-fry them for 1–2 minutes, shaking occasionally, until toasted and fragrant.

2 Transfer the spices to a mortar and bash them with a pestle or blitz them in a mini food processor until they are crushed but not powdered. Add the oil, chilli flakes and coriander and stir well to combine.

3 Working with one poppadum at a time, dip a pastry brush in the oil and spice mixture and use it to lightly coat the surface of the poppadum.

4 Put the poppadum on a large dinner plate and microwave on high for 40–50 seconds, or following the packet instructions, until it has puffed up and doubled in size. Keep an eye on it because it will burn if it's cooked for too long.

5 Put the hot poppadum on a warm plate lined with kitchen paper, then repeat the painting and cooking process with all of the poppadums. Serve immediately with chutneys.

Parathas

DIFFICULTY: 🍳🍳

EQUIPMENT: Large, heavy skillet or griddle pan

MAKES: 8

PREP TIME: 30 minutes, plus 20 minutes resting

COOKING TIME: about 25 minutes

A paratha is a delicious flaky-textured flat bread from southern India that is more indulgent than a naan or roti, and as such it's an all-day kind of bread that can be enjoyed with equal gusto alongside sugary syrups or spicy savoury sauces. The technique for making it is similar to the one used for making flaky or rough puff pastry, in that it is folded several times with butter to create layers, or lamination. This requires a bit of patience, but since the bread is unleavened (made without yeast), it is still much quicker to make than many breads since it doesn't have to prove. So roll your sleeves up and give it a bash – I promise it's worth it.

50g/2oz/½ cup strong white bread flour, plus extra for dusting

250g/9oz/2¼ cups chapatti flour or wholemeal (whole-wheat) bread flour

pinch of salt

115g/4oz/½ cup ghee, melted

150–175ml/4–6fl oz/²/₃–³/₄ cup cold water

1 Sift the flours together into a medium bowl. Add the salt and 45ml/3 tbsp of the melted ghee. Rub the ghee into the flour to form a texture like breadcrumbs.

2 Add most of the water and mix to form a smooth dough, adding a little extra water if necessary to bind it. Tip the dough out on to a lightly floured surface and knead for a couple of minutes. Return to the bowl, cover and leave it to rest for 20 minutes.

3 Divide the dough into eight small balls. Lightly flour a surface and roll each ball into a disc measuring about 15cm/6in across. Brush the top with a little melted ghee and dust with a little white bread flour. Repeat the folding, brushing and dusting process twice more, until you have a folded triangle shape.

4 Repeat for all of the remaining balls, stacking completed ones in between sheets of greaseproof (waxed) paper.

5 Heat a large, heavy skillet or griddle pan over a medium heat.

6 On a lightly floured surface roll each triangle into a large triangle about 12.5cm/5in long. Brush with the remaining ghee and place in the hot skillet or pan, ghee side down.

7 Cook for 1–2 minutes, brush the uncooked side with a little more ghee and turn the paratha over. Cook the other side for another 1–2 minutes. The surface should be a golden colour with dark speckles.

8 Remove and keep warm while you cook the remaining triangles in the same way. Serve immediately.

French fries with chicken salt

Chicken salt – a mixture of dry seasonings – is available commercially, but it's a cinch to mix some up yourself and keep it in the store cupboard. Note: no chickens are harmed in the making of the mixture. The variety of potato used for these thin-cut fries is important – they should be floury rather than waxy. The cooking method is also critical: this recipe has two stages of frying – the initial fry at a low-ish temperature, which cooks the insides, and a second much hotter fry to crisp up the outsides. The real secret, though, is to soak the raw fries in sweetened water. I was slightly surprised by the impact this had on the finished fries!

DIFFICULTY:

EQUIPMENT: Deep-fryer or large, heavy pan suitable for deep-frying, frying basket or slotted spoon

SERVES: 4

PREP TIME: 15 minutes, plus 30 minutes soaking, and chilling

COOKING TIME: about 10 minutes

---

8 large floury potatoes, about 1.6kg/3½lb

15ml/1 tbsp corn syrup

about 3 litres/5 pints/12½ cups oil, for deep-frying

FOR THE CHICKEN SALT

5ml/1 tsp each of garlic powder and onion powder

10ml/2 tsp salt

good pinch each of ground turmeric and smoked paprika

---

1 Peel the potatoes, then cut them into 5mm/¼in-wide matchsticks. You can leave some pointy ends.

2 Mix together the ingredients for the chicken salt and set aside.

3 Mix the corn syrup with some warm water in a large bowl and add the potatoes. Cover and leave to stand for 30 minutes. Drain and pat dry in kitchen paper to remove all the excess water.

4 Put the oil in a deep-fryer or large, heavy pan suitable for deep-frying and heat it to 130ºC/266ºF. Fry the chips for 4–5 minutes until tender but still holding their shape. Scoop out with the fryer basket or a slotted spoon and drain on kitchen paper, then place in the refrigerator to cool.

5 Heat the oil to 180ºC/350ºF. Lower in the fries and cook for 5–6 minutes, until crisp and golden.

6 Drain on kitchen paper, sprinkle generously with chicken salt and serve immediately.

Naan breads

DIFFICULTY:

EQUIPMENT: Dough hook and a stand mixer (optional)

SERVES: 6

PREP TIME: 25–30 minutes, plus 45 minutes proving

COOKING TIME: about 30 minutes

150ml/¼ pint/²/₃ cup water

10g/¼oz active dry yeast

pinch of sugar

525g/1lb 5oz/4²/₃ cups strong wholemeal (whole-wheat) bread flour

generous pinch each of salt and nigella seeds

200ml/7oz/scant 1 cup natural (plain) yogurt

75ml/5 tbsp ghee, melted

4 garlic cloves, peeled and crushed

30ml/2 tbsp chopped fresh coriander (cilantro) and fresh parsley leaves

plain (all-purpose) flour, for dusting

A real staple in some parts of India, naan bakes in almost seconds in the belly of a fiery tandoor, and should be served straight out of the oven or pan, when it is crispy and warm, with a moreish garlic butter slathered over it – perfect for mopping up every last drop of curry. Obviously most domestic kitchens don't feature a tandoor or clay oven (it will work very well in a pizza oven, should you have one in your garden), but fortunately you can get very good results using a heavy frying pan set over a raging flame.

1 Warm 60ml/4 tbsp of the water until it is blood temperature in a medium bowl. Add the yeast and sugar and stir to dissolve, then leave it somewhere warm for 10 minutes or until the yeast starts to activate and bubble.

2 Meanwhile, put the flour, salt and nigella seeds into a large mixing bowl and make a well in the middle. Add the yogurt, yeast mixture and remaining water into the well.

3 Use your hands to bring the mixture together into a ball, then tip it on to a lightly floured surface and knead for about 10 minutes, until the dough is smooth and silky to touch. You could use a dough hook and a stand mixer to do this for you, in which case knead for about 5 minutes. It should bounce back at you when gently prodded.

4 Use a little of the melted ghee to grease the inside of the bowl. Place the dough into the bowl, cover with clear film (plastic wrap) and set aside in a warm place for about 45 minutes, until the dough has doubled in size.

5 Divide the dough into six small balls. Dust the surface and roll it out to an oval or classic naan teardrop shape.

6 Now you can start baking them. Heat a large (about 30cm/12in across) frying pan to an unmerciful temperature, roll the naan around a rolling pin and gently drop it into a dry pan so it falls flat on the blistering surface.

7 Cook until it starts to puff up a little and is slightly charred, about 2–3 minutes. Flip it over and cook the other side.

8 Transfer to a warm plate, cover with a clean dish towel to keep it soft and repeat the cooking process until all the naans are cooked.

9 Mix the ghee and garlic together and brush a generous amount of the mixture on one side of the cooked breads. Finish with a flourish of chopped herbs and serve immediately.

Hot sauce

DIFFICULTY:

EQUIPMENT: Barbecue, blender or stick blender, bottle

MAKES: About 250ml/ 8fl oz/1 cup

PREP TIME: 20 minutes, plus time to prepare the barbecue

COOKING TIME: 50-55 minutes

Adding a few drops of culinary lava is a sure-fire way to add a bit of spice to your life, and making your own means you can have complete control over how hot, or not, it is. If you really want to dial up the heat then go for a hotter chilli, such as Scotch bonnet or facing heaven peppers – just make sure you put the sauce into little bottles with a small opening so that you use it sparingly, drop by drop, rather than in a sudden uncontrolled squirt that might make your food inedible.

4 red Ramiro or other sweet bell peppers
10 long fresh red chillies, such as Serrano
60ml/4 tbsp white wine vinegar
30ml/2 tbsp soft dark brown sugar
30ml/2 tbsp butter
3 garlic cloves, peeled and crushed
salt and ground black pepper

1 Preheat a barbecue to smouldering embers. Wrap the peppers and chillies in a foil parcel, place on the barbecue and roast for about 30 minutes, until the chillies and peppers are softened and a little blistered and have taken on some of the smoky aromas. You could also skewer the peppers and chillies and rotate them over a naked flame or use a blowtorch to char the skins, if you don't have a barbecue on the go.

2 Once the skins are charred, place the peppers into a bag, seal and leave them to sweat for about 10 minutes.

3 Meanwhile, remove and discard the stalks from the chillies and put the bodies in a small pan. Add the remaining ingredients, including a good blast of seasoning.

4 Remove the peppers from the bag, pull away the skins and remove the stalks and seeds. Add the pepper flesh to the pan, then place over a very low heat and simmer for 20–25 minutes, until everything is completely softened.

5 Blitz the mixture in a blender or with a stick blender, then sieve it into a jug or pitcher. Pour the sauce into a clean bottle with a narrow neck and seal.

6 Keep in a cool, dark place for up to 3 months. Once opened, keep it in the refrigerator.

Home-made mustard & ketchup

DIFFICULTY:

EQUIPMENT: Airtight container, large, heavy pan with a tight-fitting lid, blender, bottles and jars

MAKES: 1 bottle of each

PREP TIME:

MUSTARD: 5 minutes, plus 2-3 days soaking

KETCHUP: 20 minutes

COOKING TIME:

MUSTARD: 0 minutes

KETCHUP: 3 hours 40 minutes

Mustard in all its interpretations is a much-loved condiment, the peppery heat of which cuts through the richness of loads of fakeaway favourites. From America to Dijon to Tewkesbury, there are many variations in strength and textures, but this one is a mild, blended, American-style mustard that goes well with most things. Ketchup, perhaps the most ubiquitous of all sauces, is the final flourish that just lifts food to that next level. Making your own ramps things up a whole other gear and will impress your mates no end, and it's easy to do using whatever tomatoes are ripe and in season.

FOR THE MUSTARD

100g/3³/₄oz/²/₃ cup yellow mustard seeds

150ml/¹/₄ pint/²/₃ cup your favourite beer

150ml/¹/₄ pint/²/₃ cup cider vinegar

5ml/1 tsp ground turmeric

15ml/1 tbsp maple syrup

good pinch of salt and cayenne pepper

FOR THE KETCHUP

2kg/4¹/₂lb ripe plum or San Marzano tomatoes (or whatever is ripe), chopped

5ml/1 tsp celery salt

3 banana shallots, peeled and finely choped

3 garlic cloves, peeled and finely crushed

5ml/1 tsp Hot Sauce (see page 130)

200ml/7fl oz/scant 1 cup malt vinegar

pinch of ground cloves

2 bay leaves

200g/7oz/scant 1 cup soft dark brown sugar

salt and ground black pepper

FOR THE MUSTARD:

1 Mix all the ingredients together in an airtight container, seal and leave to soak for 2–3 days.

2 Blend in a food processor until smooth; add a little boiling water if it is too thick. Spoon into a warm clean bottle or jar and seal tightly with a clean lid.

3 Keep in a cool, dark place for up to 3 months. Once opened, keep it in the refrigerator.

FOR THE KETCHUP:

1 Put all the ingredients except the sugar into a large, heavy pan. Slowly bring to the boil.

2 Meanwhile, preheat the oven to 110°C/225°F/Gas ¼. When the tomatoes are bubbling, pop the lid on and put into the oven for 2–3 hours, until cooked down.

3 Return the pan to the stove over a medium heat and stir in the sugar, until it has dissolved. Continue cooking for about 40 minutes, until the sauce is thick and reduced.

4 Fish out the bay leaves, then pour the hot ketchup into a blender and blend until it's super smooth.

5 Pass the ketchup through a fine sieve into a clean jug or pitcher and decant it into warm sterilised jars or bottles, and seal with clean lids.

6 It will keep in a cool, dry place for up to 3 months. Once opened, keep it in the refrigerator.

Indian pickles & chutneys

When the Southern Indian thali is served it usually arrives at your table with a variety of sweet, sour and spicy pickles and chutneys, which provide contrast to the rich flavours of the meat, fish or dhals. This awesome foursome covers all your curry needs, whether you want to get the party going by slathering them on poppadums or mix and match with your other dishes. Feel free to up the heat as much as you dare! There's also more than enough to go round here and most will keep in a sealed container for at least 3 days, so you can double up the quantities and prepare ahead of time if you're having a party.

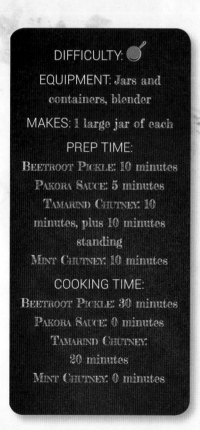

DIFFICULTY:

EQUIPMENT: Jars and containers, blender

MAKES: 1 large jar of each

PREP TIME:
Beetroot Pickle: 10 minutes
Pakora Sauce: 5 minutes
Tamarind Chutney: 10 minutes, plus 10 minutes standing
Mint Chutney: 10 minutes

COOKING TIME:
Beetroot Pickle: 30 minutes
Pakora Sauce: 0 minutes
Tamarind Chutney: 20 minutes
Mint Chutney: 0 minutes

FOR THE BEETROOT PICKLE

6 beetroots (beets)
good pinch of chilli powder
2.5ml/½ tsp ground turmeric
400ml/14fl oz/1²/₃ cups cider vinegar
150g/5oz/³/₄ cup caster (superfine) sugar
75ml/5 tbsp mustard oil
15ml/1 tbsp black mustard seeds
salt and ground black pepper

FOR THE PAKORA SAUCE

1 red onion, peeled and finely chopped
15ml/1 tbsp mint sauce
175ml/6fl oz/³/₄ cup natural (plain) yogurt
juice of 1 lime
pinch of chilli powder
15ml/1 tbsp mango chutney
pinch of onion seeds
15ml/1 tbsp Home-made Ketchup (see page 131)
15ml/1 tbsp finely grated fresh root ginger
salt and ground black pepper

FOR THE TAMARIND CHUTNEY

100g/3³/₄oz prepared tamarind pulp (made according to packet instructions)
5ml/1 tsp cumin seeds, toasted
2 garlic cloves, peeled and crushed
30ml/2 tbsp soft light brown sugar
pinch of chilli powder
5ml/1 tsp onion seeds
150g/5oz cherry tomatoes, quartered
15ml/1 tbsp raisins
salt and ground black pepper

3 Season with a little salt and pepper and pour into a warmed sterilised jar (see page 16) and seal. Store for up to 3 months.

FOR THE PAKORA SAUCE:

Mix all the ingredients together in a large bowl, check and adjust the seasoning and decant into a clean container. Refrigerate for up to 3 days.

FOR THE TAMARIND CHUTNEY:

1 Put all the ingredients apart from the raisins and seasoning in a small, heavy pan over a low heat. Slowly bring to the simmer and cook for about 20 minutes, until thickened.

2 Stir in the raisins and salt and pepper and leave to stand for 10 minutes to allow the raisins to swell.

3 Decant into a clean container and refrigerate for up to 5 days.

FOR THE MINT CHUTNEY:

1 Put all the ingredients apart from the seasoning into a blender. Blend until smooth and vibrant green, then season with a little salt and pepper — it should have a sweet and sour tang.

2 Decant into a clean container and refrigerate for up to 3 days.

FOR THE MINT CHUTNEY:

large bunch of fresh mint, leaves picked

large bunch of fresh coriander, leaves picked

2 fresh green chillies, seeded and finely chopped

15ml/1 tbsp lime juice

45ml/3 tbsp prepared tamarind pulp (made according to packet instructions)

2 garlic cloves, peeled and crushed

15ml/1 tbsp finely grated fresh root ginger

salt and ground black pepper

FOR THE BEETROOT PICKLE:

1 Wearing a pair of rubber gloves, remove the skin from the beetroots with a vegetable peeler. Cut into thin matchsticks and put them in a medium pan.

2 Add the other ingredients, apart from the salt and pepper, stir to combine and simmer for about 30 minutes, until the beetroot is tender.

Triple chocolate brownies

DIFFICULTY: 🍳

EQUIPMENT: Microwave (optional), 20 x 25cm/8 x 10in brownie tin (pan), hand-held or stand mixer or whisk

SERVES: 1-12!

PREP TIME: 15 minutes

COOKING TIME: 35-40 minutes

150g/5oz dark (bittersweet) chocolate (70% cocoa solids), chopped

150g/5oz milk chocolate (30% cocoa solids), chopped

175g/6oz/³/₄ cup butter, softened, plus a little extra for greasing

375g/13oz/1²/₃ cups soft light brown sugar

2 eggs

100g/3³/₄oz/scant 1 cup ground almonds

30ml/2 tbsp unsweetened cocoa powder

5ml/1 tsp salt

7.5ml/1¹/₂ tsp vanilla extract

50g/¹/₂ cup chopped almonds

FOR DECORATING

25g/1oz dark (bittersweet) chocolate (70% cocoa solids), chopped

25g/1oz milk chocolate (30% cocoa solids), chopped

25g/1oz white chocolate, chopped

Originating in the USA and named after their colour (like their lesser-known sister, the blondie), these brownies really are manna from heaven for chocolate connoisseurs. Containing both dark and milk chocolate, they have a chewy texture on the outside, created by the use of soft light brown sugar, but inside lies a gooey heart of darkness that simply can't be beaten by store-bought versions. The secret is to be super-vigilant when they are baking, just a minute or two too long in the oven and the soft centre will disappear. Make sure they still squish slightly when you're testing for doneness.

1 Grease a brownie tin with a little butter and line the base with a sheet of baking parchment. Preheat the oven to 160°C/325°F/Gas 3.

2 Set aside 75g/2¹/₂oz each of the dark and milk chocolate for stirring in later. Put the remaining chocolate in a heatproof bowl and set over a pan of barely simmering water, making sure the bowl doesn't touch the water. Leave until the chocolate has melted, then stir gently to mix. Or, melt the chocolate in the microwave on low, in short bursts, stirring between bursts. Set aside, but ensure it remains liquid.

3 Beat the butter and sugar with a hand-held or stand mixer or with a hand whisk for about 2 minutes, until light and creamy. Add the eggs one by one, beating well between additions.

4 Fold in the ground almonds, cocoa powder, slightly cooled melted chocolate, salt and vanilla. Add the remaining chopped chocolate and the chopped almonds and fold through. Scrape the mixture into the prepared tin and push it to the edges.

5 Bake on the middle shelf of the preheated oven for 30–35 minutes – it should be squishy with a few hairline cracks on the surface.

6 Remove from the oven and leave to cool in the tin on a wire rack.

7 When the brownies are completely cool, melt the reserved dark and milk chocolates and the white chocolate in separate small bowls and get creative drizzling them over the top of the brownies. Slice into squares and serve cold.

Doughnuts

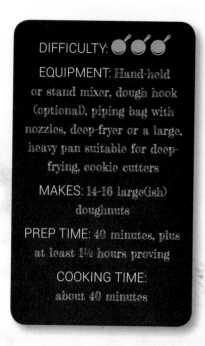

DIFFICULTY: 🍳🍳🍳

EQUIPMENT: Hand-held or stand mixer, dough hook (optional), piping bag with nozzles, deep-fryer or a large, heavy pan suitable for deep-frying, cookie cutters

MAKES: 14-16 large(ish) doughnuts

PREP TIME: 40 minutes, plus at least 1½ hours proving

COOKING TIME: about 40 minutes

10g/¼oz active dried yeast

115g/4oz/½ cup soft light brown sugar, plus a pinch for the yeast

250ml/8fl oz/1 cup full-fat (whole) milk, warmed to blood temperature

175/6oz/¾ cup butter, softened

5 eggs

oil, for deep-frying

725g/1lb 10oz/6½ cups plain (all-purpose) flour

pinch of salt

golden granulated sugar, for dredging

raspberry jam and crème patissiere (see below), for filling

FOR THE CRÈME PATISSIERE

4 egg yolks

60ml/4 tbsp sugar

300ml/½ pint/1¼ cups full-fat (whole) milk

30ml/2 tbsp plain (all-purpose) flour

15ml/1 tbsp cornflour (cornstarch)

5ml/1 tsp vanilla bean paste or extract

The doughnut is a well-travelled colonial food that made its way to the Americas via Dutch settlers in New Amsterdam (New York). Now a symbol of the USA, they can be ring-shaped and glazed or near-spherical, and contain fillings, ranging from jam to lemon curd to toffee sauce. Making your own is fun and gives you scope to change things up and try out different combinations. There are a variety of flavours that can be used inside, outside and through your doughnuts, including sugars flavoured with vanilla, cinnamon, fennel and even lavender. This recipe makes lots, so why not throw a doughnut party and get guests to fill their own?

1 First, make the crème patissiere. Beat the egg yolks and sugar in a hand-held or stand mixer for about 5 minutes, until pale and creamy.

2 Bring the milk to a gentle simmer in a small pan. Whisk the flour into the egg mixture, then add the warmed milk and the vanilla, whisking all the time. Pour the mixture into the milk pan and simmer gently over a low heat for 8–10 minutes, stirring all the time, until it coats the back of a spoon.

3 Transfer to a small bowl, cover the surface with clear film (plastic wrap) and chill until ready to use.

4 Blend the yeast with the pinch of sugar and 30ml/2 tbsp of the warm milk, then leave it somewhere warm for 10 minutes or until the yeast starts to activate and bubble.

5 Cream together the butter and sugar in a large bowl with a hand mixer or in a stand mixer for about 5 minutes, until smooth and creamy. Beat the eggs in one at a time, mixing well between additions.

6 Slowly add the yeast mixture and the rest of the milk, then fold in the flour and salt. The dough should come together now into a smooth and slightly sticky dough. A little flour can be added if the dough is too sticky.

7 Tip the dough on to a lightly floured surface and knead for about 10 minutes, until smooth and elastic. You could use a dough hook and a food processor to do this for you, in which case knead for about 5 minutes.

8 Return the dough to the bowl and cover with a clean dish towel. You can now pop it in the fridge for a slow prove or accelerate it by leaving the bowl in a warm place for about an hour, until doubled in size.

9 Prepare some baking sheets by lining them with baking paper.

10 Knock back (punch down) the dough to remove the air, then tip it out on to a lightly floured surface and knead gently for about 2 minutes.

11 Roll out the dough until it is about 2cm/¾in thick. Using a round 6cm/2½in cookie cutter stamp out discs and place these on the prepared baking sheets. Reshape any remaining dough. Cover loosely with clear film and leave in a warm place for about 30 minutes, until risen.

12 When the dough balls are ready, heat the oil to 180ºC/350ºF in a deep-fryer or large, heavy pan suitable for deep-frying. Test whether it is ready by putting a piece of dough in the oil. If it spits and fizzes, the oil is ready.

13 Using a flat spatula and working in batches, lower the balls into the hot oil. Fry for about 3–4 minutes, then flip them and cook the other side for another 3–4 minutes.

14 You should have a nice blonde ring around the circumference of the doughnut and a deep golden colour on the top and bottom.

15 Remove and drain well on kitchen paper while you cook the remaining doughnuts in the same way. Dredge the hot doughnuts in sugar and leave to cool.

16 Make an incision in each doughnut with the piping bag nozzle and insert about 5ml/1 tsp jam and/or crème patissiere into the centre.

COOK'S TIP
Some recipes develop sourdough-like notes in the doughnuts by proving the dough overnight. This is entirely optional, although doing so has the advantage that you can prepare your dough in advance.

DIFFICULTY:

EQUIPMENT: Piping bag with a star-shaped nozzle or a churros maker, deep-fryer or a large, heavy pan suitable for deep-frying

SERVES: 4

PREP TIME: 15 minutes

COOKING TIME: 10-15 minutes

Piping-hot, sugar-coated doughnuts dipped in a thick, velvety dark chocolate sauce are irresistible at any time of the day — in Spain and the Iberian Peninsula they are a popular breakfast treat, as well as being the hottest ticket in town at music festivals and street-food events. You can play around with different flavours of sugar when you make your own, but the Spanish and Portuguese generally prefer either plain granulated sugar or a little bit of cinnamon mixed through. A lot of recipes don't contain eggs, but I find that adding a couple gives the *churros* a richer, more structured finish. To make the churros in an authentic-looking way, use either a churros maker or a piping bag fitted with a large, star-shaped nozzle. You can make them long or crazy curly if you wish, but generally they should all be slightly different.

FOR THE SAUCE

200g/7oz dark (bittersweet) chocolate (70% cocoa solids), broken into pieces

100ml/3½fl oz/scant ½ cup double (heavy) cream

100ml/3½fl oz/scant ½ cup full-fat (whole) milk

45ml/3 tbsp golden (light corn) syrup

tiny pinch of salt

FOR THE CHURROS

300ml/½ pint/1¼ cups boiling water

60ml/4 tbsp melted butter

5ml/1 tsp vanilla bean paste or extract

325g/11oz/scant 3 cups plain (all-purpose) flour

5ml/1 tsp baking powder

pinch of salt

2 egg yolks

oil, for deep-frying

FOR SPRINKLING

50g/2oz/¼ cup golden granulated sugar

7.5/1½ tsp ground cinnamon

Preheat the oven to 120°C/250°F/ Gas ½. Prepare the sauce by putting all the ingredients in a small pan and placing it over a gentle heat. Stir until the chocolate melts. Set aside and keep warm.

To make the batter for the churros, mix the water, butter and vanilla bean paste together. Sift the flour and baking powder into a large mixing bowl. Make a well in the centre of the flour and pour in the butter mixture. Add the salt and bring the mixture together.

Heat the oil to 160°C/325°F in a deep-fryer or a large, heavy pan suitable for deep-frying.

Scrape the batter into a churros maker or piping bag. Squeeze out lengths measuring about 7.5cm/3in into the hot oil, using a blunt knife if you want to cut them off. Don't overcrowd the pan — you'll probably need to work in batches.

Cook the churros for 3–4 minutes, until golden and crisp, then scoop

out with a slotted spoon and drain on kitchen paper. Repeat the process until all of the batter has been used up.

Mix the sugar and cinnamon in a shallow dish. Roll the warm churros in the sugar and serve immediately with the warmed chocolate sauce.

Waffles

DIFFICULTY ●●

EQUIPMENT: Waffle iron or electric waffle maker

SERVES: 2-4

PREP TIME: 10 minutes

COOKING TIME: 5-10 minutes

Waffles are conveniently versatile carriers for all manner of toppings – from crispy bacon and maple syrup to whipped cream, ice cream and fresh fruit, or chocolate or toffee sauce – and whether you chow down on them for breakfast, brunch or dessert is entirely up to you. You can make them at home with a waffle iron for authenticity but there are many electric waffle makers on the market, which are very easy to use. Without either of these the waffle becomes more of a fluffy pancake. The secret to making good waffles is to have plenty of butter and a little fine cornmeal in the batter as these will give extra crunch – much like the base on a deep pan pizza.

oil, for greasing
225g/8oz/2 cups plain (all-purpose) flour
7.5ml/1½ tsp baking powder
2.5ml/½ tsp bicarbonate of soda (baking soda)
45ml/3 tbsp caster (superfine) sugar
15ml/1 tbsp fine cornmeal
good pinch of salt
2 eggs
300ml/½ pint/1¼ cups buttermilk, at room temperature
45ml/3 tbsp melted butter
15ml/1 tbsp vanilla bean paste

TO SERVE
vanilla ice cream
roasted unsalted pistachios
raspberries
maple syrup
icing (confectioners') sugar, for dusting

1 Oil the waffle iron, then preheat it, following the manufacturer's instructions. Preheat the oven to a low holding temperature, about 110°C/225°F/Gas ¼.

2 Sift the flour, baking powder and bicarbonate of soda into a large bowl. Add the sugar, cornmeal and a good pinch of salt. Make a well in the centre.

3 Mix the eggs, buttermilk, melted butter and vanilla bean paste together and pour into the dry mixture. Whisk until the batter is smooth.

4 Ladle some of the batter into the waffle iron and spread it out evenly. Cook for about 2 minutes, until crisp and golden. Transfer to plate and keep warm in the preheated oven while you make the rest of the waffles in the same way.

5 Serve each with a scoop of ice cream, some pistachios, raspberries and maple syrup, all dusted with icing sugar.

FOR THE PASTRY

275g/10oz/2½ cups plain (all-purpose) flour, plus lots extra for dusting

200ml/7fl oz/scant 1 cup cold water

pinch of salt

225g/8oz/1 cup butter, softened, plus extra for greasing

FOR THE FILLING

60ml/4 tbsp plain (all-purpose) flour

500ml/17fl oz/generous 2 cups full-fat (whole) milk

1 cinnamon stick, snapped

250g/9oz/1¼ cups caster (superfine) sugar

100ml/3½fl oz/scant ½ cup water

6 egg yolks, beaten (see Cook's Tip)

5ml/1 tsp vanilla bean paste

icing (confectioners') sugar and ground cinnamon, for dusting (optional)

COOK'S TIP

You will have some leftover egg whites after you have separated the eggs for the custard. You can either use them up straight away to clarify a consommé or make a meringue, or you can lightly whisk and then freeze them. They will keep, stored in plastic containers, for up to 3 months.

Portuguese custard tarts

DIFFICULTY: 🍳🍳🍳

EQUIPMENT: Mixer with a dough hook (optional), 2 x 12-hole cupcake tins (pans)

MAKES: 24

PREP TIME: 45 minutes

COOKING TIME: 15 minutes

These iconic tarts, known as *pastel de nata* in their native Lisbon, are often enjoyed for breakfast in bars with a shot of treacly black coffee or even a cheeky beer. Deceptively simple to look at, with their buttery pastry casings and burnished custard fillings, they are undoubtedly quite challenging to perfect, but don't let that put you off: if you don't fancy making the pastry yourself you can always use a really good bought all-butter puff pastry instead – it's the freshness that comes from baking them at home that really elevates them above bland supermarket affairs, so rest assured they'll still taste marvellous.

1 To make the pastry, combine the flour, water and salt until it comes together in a ball. If you have a mixer with a dough hook then so much the better.

2 Tip the dough out on to a well-floured surface and form it into a rough rectangle. Wrap it in clear film (plastic wrap) and place it flat in the fridge for about 15 minutes.

3 Flour the surface and roll the dough out to a square measuring about 40 x 40cm/16 x 16in. Dust off any excess flour from the surface.

4 Gently spread about one-third of the butter over the pastry, leaving a 2.5cm/1in border all around. Use a floured palette knife to help you fold about one-third of one side of the pastry over, and then fold the opposing buttered side on top.

5 Use plenty of flour to help you rotate the pastry through 90 degrees so the fold is facing you. Roll the pastry once more to a 40 x 40cm/16 x 16in square and add one-third of the butter. Fold into thirds again. Rotate the pastry through 90 degrees and roll it out to approximately 45 x 55cm/18 x 22in.

6 Trim off any excess pastry so you have a neat rectangle. Cover in the remaining softened butter.

7 Roll the pastry up into a tight sausage shape (brushing away any excess flour). Trim the ends, then slice it in two, cover loosely with clear film and refrigerate for at least 3 hours.

8 Lightly grease 2 x 12-hole cupcake tins (pans) with a little butter.

9 To make the filling, mix the flour with about 60ml/4 tbsp of the milk. Heat the rest of the milk with the cinnamon in a medium pan until just boiling. Add the flour mixture to the milk, then remove from the heat.

10 In another pan, stir the sugar and water over a gentle heat until dissolved, then boil for 2–3 minutes, until a syrup forms.

11 Add the sugar syrup to the milk mixture in a thin, steady stream, stirring constantly. Strain through a sieve and allow to cool completely.

12 Stir in the egg yolks and vanilla and transfer the custard to a jug or pitcher ready for pouring.

13 Remove the pastry from the fridge and slice it into rounds measuring about 2.5cm/1in in diameter. Place the rounds into the cupcake tins with the flaky laminations facing upwards. Leave at room temperature for about 10–15 minutes, until the pastry softens a bit.

14 Preheat the oven to its highest setting – higher than 240ºC/475ºF/Gas 9 if possible.

15 Using a little bowl of cold water to wet your thumbs, manipulate the pastry into the tins to create nice deep holes for your custard to sit in, making sure the pastry goes right up to the top of the sides of the tin.

16 Three-quarters fill each pastry case with custard mixture and bake in the preheated oven for 8–10 minutes, until a few black scorch marks appear on the surface of the custard and the pastry is golden. Keep watching them – you don't want the pastry to burn.

17 Remove from the oven and leave to cool slightly, then slip them out of the tins and sprinkle with a little icing sugar and ground cinnamon if you like. Eat warm.

Deep-fried Crunchie™ bars

DIFFICULTY:

EQUIPMENT: Deep-fryer or a large, heavy pan suitable for deep-frying

SERVES: 4

PREP TIME: 20 minutes, plus 30 minutes freezing

COOKING TIME: 2-4 minutes

The origins of this delicious, though admittedly rather unsophisticated, treat lie in the East Coast of Scotland, where the bracing winds off the North Sea mean dietary requirements run a little on the higher side of the recommended daily allowances of calories. Health food this isn't, but it sure does taste good – maybe just go for a bracing walk after eating one. There are no hard-and-fast rules when it comes to deep-frying bars of chocolate, so play around and try any you fancy. The reason I chose a Crunchie™ is down to its crisp honeycomb centre, which is a great contrast to the soft chocolate and crispy batter.

4 fun or snack-sized Crunchie™ bars

200ml/7fl oz/scant 1 cup milk

150g/5oz/1¼ cups self-raising (self-rising) flour

2.5ml/½ tsp salt

oil, for deep-frying

unsweetened cocoa powder and icing (confectioners') sugar, for dusting

vanilla ice cream, to serve

1 Place the Crunchie™ bars in the freezer for about 30 minutes to make sure they are properly cold.

2 Take 30ml/2 tbsp each of milk and flour and put them on separate small side plates.

3 Sift together the remaining flour and the salt into a medium bowl. Make a well in the middle and gradually stir in the remaining milk to make a smooth batter. Set aside for 5–10 minutes in the fridge.

4 Heat the oil to 180ºC/350ºF in a deep-fryer or large, heavy pan suitable for deep-frying. Test whether it is ready by putting a trickle of the batter in the oil. If it spits and fizzes, the oil is ready.

5 Dip the Crunchie™ bars into the cold milk, then into the flour, then into the batter and carefully lower them into the hot oil. Cook for about 2 minutes until crisp and golden. Remove with a slotted spoon and drain on kitchen paper. You may need to work in batches.

6 Dust with a little cocoa powder and icing sugar and serve immediately with vanilla ice cream.

Mango Lassi & Salty Lassi

DIFFICULTY:

EQUIPMENT: Blender

SERVES: Each serves 2

PREP TIME: 5 minutes, plus
30 minutes freezing

COOKING TIME: N/a

Essentially Indian milkshakes, lassis are wonder drinks that help replenish salt, sugar and water levels in the body and, when drunk at mealtimes, can aid digestion. Here are two versions: one fresh and fruity, the other distinctly savoury and salty, with a kick from fresh chilli. If you are struggling to find good mangoes then frozen mango cubes are a worthy substitute. What's more, you can store the latter in your freezer so you have a fresh drink in front of you in seconds – just omit the ice cubes if you are using them.

FOR MANGO LASSI

450g/1lb/2 cups natural (plain) yogurt

100ml/3½fl oz/scant ½ cup milk

about 15ml/1 tbsp sugar

1 mango, peeled and chopped or pulped, or several frozen mango cubes

ice cubes (if using fresh mango)

FOR SALTY LASSI

500g/1lb 2oz/generous 2 cups natural (plain) yogurt

100ml/3½fl oz/scant ½ cup milk

1 fresh green chilli, seeded and finely chopped

5ml/1 tsp cumin seeds, roasted and crushed

30ml/2 tbsp chopped fresh mint leaves

about a pinch of salt

ice cubes

1 Before making either lassi, put the glasses/cups in the freezer for about 30 minutes to chill.

2 Combine all the ingredients for either lassi in a food blender until smooth and combined, then taste and adjust the sweetness or saltiness to suit.

3 Pour into the chilled glasses and slurp immediately.

VARIATIONS

Sheep's or goat's yogurt and milk work really well in place of cow's or, if you are vegan, try making them with a little silken tofu and almond milk or some raw coconut yogurt and coconut milk.

Smoothies

DIFFICULTY: ⬤

EQUIPMENT: Blender

SERVES: Each serves 1

PREP TIME: 5 minutes

COOKING TIME: N/a

Sold for a fortune at gyms, cafés, street-food markets and specialist bars all over the world, smoothies are by far the simplest and quickest of takeaway 'foods' to prepare at home and are perhaps one of the healthiest, too. Frozen fruit chunks or mixed berries produce an icy, slurpy finish while adding a little oatmeal gives more fibre. Here are two recipes, one for breakfast and one for whenever you need a refreshing and energising pick-me-up.

1 Whichever smoothie you decide to make, the method is the same. Place all the ingredients in a blender.

2 Blend until smooth. Pour into a tall glass and top with a few berries or mango. Drink straight away.

FOR THE BREAKFAST SMOOTHIE

½ small ripe mango, peeled and chopped into chunks

1 banana, peeled and chopped into chunks

juice of 1 orange

5ml/1 tsp golden linseeds

15ml/1 tbsp porridge oats

5ml/1 tsp honey

200ml/7fl oz/scant 1 cup almond or other milk

FOR THE MIXED BERRY SMOOTHIE

115g/4oz/1 cup frozen mixed berries

30ml/2 tbsp unblanched almonds

5ml/1 tsp honey

200ml/7fl oz/scant 1 cup almond or other milk

Index

© Fergal Connolly

Fergal Connolly has asserted his moral right to be identified as the author of this work

Photography by Nicki Dowey

All rights reserved. No part of this publication may be reproduced or stored in a retrieval system or transmitted, in any form or by any means, electronic, mechanical, photocopying, recording or otherwise, without prior permission in writing from Haynes Publishing.

First published in July 2018

A catalogue record for this book is available from the British Library

ISBN 978 1 78521 177 5

Library of Congress control no. 2017949632

Published by Haynes Publishing, Sparkford, Yeovil, Somerset BA22 7JJ, UK.
Tel: 01963 440635
www.haynes.com

Haynes North America Inc., 859 Lawrence Drive, Newbury Park, California 91320, USA.

Printed in Malaysia